CONTENTS

Digital Dummies' Guide to CYBER SAFETY

A Handbook for Secure Online Living

PRATYUSHA VEMURI

ISBN 979-8-89186-520-4

INTRODUCTION: UNDERSTANDING THE LANDSCAPE

The Digital Era and Cyber Threats

In an age where technology and connectivity are woven into the fabric of our lives, the digital landscape has become both a realm of convenience and a breeding ground for malicious intent. The onset of the digital era has revolutionized the way we work, communicate, and interact with the world. However, alongside these advancements, a lurking shadow has emerged - the world of cyber threats and frauds.

The Proliferation of Devices and Data

The first key factor in understanding the rise of cyber threats in the digital era is the proliferation of devices and the digitization of data. In the past, our interactions with technology were limited to a few desktop computers, but today, we carry powerful smartphones, tablets, and wearables that are constantly connected to the internet. This has created a vast and interconnected ecosystem where information flows freely between devices and systems. While this connectivity has improved our lives in countless ways, it has also created an expansive attack surface for cybercriminals to exploit.

Every text message sent, email received, or financial transaction made generates a trail of data that can be manipulated or stolen by malicious actors. The massive volumes of data generated in the digital era have become valuable commodities in the underground economy, driving cybercriminals to seek out opportunities to exploit vulnerabilities in systems and applications.

Interconnectivity and Vulnerabilities

Interconnectivity is another critical aspect of the digital era that has given rise to cyber threats. Our homes, workplaces, and critical infrastructure are now connected through the Internet of Things (IoT), making our daily lives more efficient and convenient. However, this interconnectivity also means that a security breach in one area can have far-reaching consequences.

For example, a vulnerability in a smart home device could potentially be exploited to gain access to personal information, and from there, cybercriminals could pivot to compromise a larger network and gain access to critical financial information too. By exploiting this vulnerability, they could gain access to the homeowner's security camera feeds, door locks, and alarm systems. This breach not only compromises the individual's privacy but also poses physical security risks as unauthorized persons can enter the home. Children are increasingly becoming targets for identity theft. A cybercriminal could exploit a child's personal information to open fraudulent accounts, including credit cards and bank accounts. Since minors don't typically monitor their credit reports, such theft can go undetected for years, and the child's financial future may be compromised. Similarly attacks on critical infrastructure, such as power grids or transportation systems, can disrupt entire regions, causing economic and social upheaval.

Motivations of Cybercriminals

Understanding the motivations of cybercriminals is crucial in comprehending the scale and diversity of cyber threats. While some cybercriminals are motivated by financial gain, others are driven by ideology, espionage, or political objectives. The anonymity offered by the digital realm allows criminals to operate with relative impunity, making it an attractive option for those seeking to exploit vulnerabilities for various purposes.

Financially motivated cybercriminals engage in activities like ransomware attacks, where they encrypt a victim's data and demand a ransom for its release. These criminals often operate within well-organized, underground networks and can generate substantial profits. Meanwhile, state-sponsored hackers may target critical infrastructure or steal sensitive government information to gain a strategic advantage in international politics. Hacktivists use their skills to advance social or political causes, often through defacement or disruption of websites and online services.

The Evolution of Cyber Threats

Cyber threats have evolved from mere nuisances to highly organized and well-funded criminal endeavors. Advanced Persistent Threat (APT) groups, which are often state-sponsored or state-affiliated, employ sophisticated techniques to infiltrate and remain undetected within targeted systems for extended periods. These groups possess significant resources, including top-tier talent, funding, and access to cutting-edge technology, making them formidable adversaries.

Additionally, the emergence of the dark web, a hidden part of the internet where illegal activities thrive, has further fueled the growth of cybercrime. Here, cybercriminals can buy and sell stolen data, hacking tools, and even hire hackers-for-hire services, enabling them to carry out increasingly complex and damaging attacks.

In conclusion, as technology permeates every facet of our lives, cyber threats have grown in scope and sophistication. The digital era has brought unparalleled convenience and connectivity, but it has also exposed us to new and evolving risks. In the subsequent chapters, we will delve deeper into the specific types of cyber threats, the mechanisms employed by cybercriminals, and the strategies for mitigating these risks in our interconnected world.

Why Cybersecurity Matters

The growing dependence on technology has bestowed numerous benefits upon us, but it has also opened doors to vulnerabilities that can be exploited with devastating consequences. Cybersecurity, once relegated to the realm of IT departments, has now become a concern that should occupy the minds of individuals, organizations, and governments alike.

The Stakes Are High

The significance of cybersecurity cannot be overstated. It's not just about protecting sensitive data; it's about safeguarding our way of life. In an era where our identities, social interactions, and economic transactions are increasingly digital, the stakes have never been higher.

Consider the ramifications of a single cyber breach. Personal identities are exposed, leading to identity theft, financial fraud, and emotional distress. For organizations, a breach can result in astronomical financial losses, damage to reputation, and legal liabilities. The compromise of critical infrastructure, such as power grids or healthcare systems, poses immediate threats to public safety and national security.

The Ripple Effects of Cyber Incidents - Consumers

Cyber incidents have far-reaching consequences that extend beyond the initial breach. The ripple effects can be profound and long-lasting.

Consumers, like organizations and governments, are not immune to the ripple effects of cyber incidents. The consequences of cyberattacks and breaches can have significant and direct implications for individuals. Here's how consumers can be impacted:

Financial Loss:

- **Stolen Financial Information:** If a consumer's financial information, such as credit card details or bank account credentials, is compromised in a data breach, it can lead to unauthorized transactions and financial loss.
- **Identity Theft:** Cybercriminals can use stolen personal information to commit identity theft, opening fraudulent accounts or making unauthorized purchases in the victim's name.

Privacy Invasion:

- **Data Exposure:** Consumers entrust organizations with their personal data, and when that data is exposed in a breach, it can lead to a significant invasion of privacy. Private information, from medical records to personal photos, can be exposed without consent.
- **Online Privacy Concerns:** Consumers may become more cautious about their online activities, which can lead to a reluctance to engage with digital services due to concerns about privacy and data security.

Psychological Impact:

- **Emotional Distress:** Falling victim to a cyber incident can cause emotional distress and anxiety. The knowledge that personal information has been compromised can lead to feelings of violation and vulnerability.
- **Cyberbullying and Online Harassment:** Cybercriminals may exploit personal information to engage in cyberbullying or harassment, further impacting the psychological well-being of consumers.

Reputation Damage:

- **Online Presence Exploitation:** In some cases, cybercriminals may use stolen information to impersonate consumers online, potentially damaging their online reputation or relationships.
- **Loss of Trust:** Similar to organizations, consumers may lose trust in the entities that failed to protect their data, impacting their future engagement with those services.

Inconvenience and Time Investment:

- **Resolution Efforts:** Dealing with the aftermath of a cyber incident can be time-consuming and inconvenient. Consumers may need to contact financial institutions, update account information, or file reports to resolve issues stemming from the breach.

Educational Awareness:

- **Digital Literacy:** Cyber incidents can serve as a wake-up call for consumers, emphasizing the importance of digital literacy and cybersecurity awareness. Individuals may become more cautious in their online behavior and proactive in safeguarding their digital lives.

Cyber Insurance Consideration:

- **Insurance Needs:** After experiencing the repercussions of a cyber incident, consumers may consider investing in cyber insurance to protect themselves from future risks.

The Ripple Effects of Cyber Incidents - Corporates

- **Financial Repercussions:** The direct financial costs of a cyberattack can be crippling. Organizations may need to pay for forensic investigations, legal fees, and regulatory fines. Additionally, they may suffer from the loss of revenue due to downtime or the cost of recovering from data loss.
- **Erosion of Trust:** Trust is a fragile commodity, and a cyber breach shatters it. Customers, clients, and partners may lose faith in an organization's ability to protect their data. This erosion of trust can lead to a loss of business and long-term damage to an organization's reputation.
- **Intellectual Property Theft:** In the corporate world, intellectual property theft is a grave concern. Cybercriminals may steal valuable trade secrets, research, or proprietary software. This theft can undermine a company's competitive advantage and future innovations.
- **National Security Implications:** At the government level, the compromise of sensitive data or critical infrastructure can have profound national security implications. State-sponsored cyberattacks, for example, can disrupt essential services, compromise military secrets, or manipulate public opinion.

Real-World Examples and Case Studies: Illustrating the Importance of Cybersecurity

To underscore the urgency of cybersecurity, let's examine a few real-world examples:

- **Equifax Data Breach (2017):** The Equifax breach is one of the most significant data breaches in history. Hackers exploited a vulnerability in Equifax's website software, exposing the personal data of approximately 147 million individuals. This massive breach had severe consequences, including financial losses, identity theft, and legal consequences for Equifax. The incident serves as a stark reminder of the far-reaching impacts of inadequate cybersecurity measures. [Source](https://www.equifax.com/personal/data-breach/)

- **WannaCry Ransomware Attack (2017):** The WannaCry ransomware attack was a global cybersecurity incident that impacted over 200,000 computers across 150 countries. Hospitals, transportation systems, and businesses were disrupted as a result of this large-scale attack. WannaCry encrypted victims' files and demanded ransom payments in Bitcoin for decryption. This attack highlighted the critical importance of cybersecurity in ensuring public safety and protecting critical infrastructure. [Source] (https://www.cisa.gov/wannacry)

- **SolarWinds Cyberattack (2020):** The SolarWinds cyberattack was a highly sophisticated and stealthy supply chain attack that compromised several U.S. government agencies and private companies. The attackers infiltrated SolarWinds, a prominent IT management software provider, and used the company's software updates to distribute malware to its customers. The breach went undetected for months, showcasing the evolving tactics of modern cyber threats. This incident underscores the need for robust cybersecurity measures throughout the supply chain. [Source](https://www.fireeye.com/blog/threat-research/2020/12/evasive-attacker-leverages-solarwinds-supply-chain-compromises-with-sunburst-backdoor.html)

- **Indian Banking Sector Cyber Attacks:** India has witnessed several cyberattacks targeting its banking sector. In 2016, the infamous cyber heist on the Bangladesh Bank revealed vulnerabilities in the SWIFT messaging system. Cybercriminals attempted to siphon off nearly $1 billion but were thwarted, emphasizing the need for stronger cybersecurity defenses in the banking sector. [Source](https://www.reuters.com/article/us-cyber-heist-bangladesh-timeline/timeline-the-1-billion-cyber-heist-that-shook-the-banking-world-idUSKBN17N1GT)

There are also exponential rising frauds for Consumers too.

- **Digital Payment Scams:** With the increasing popularity of digital payments and mobile wallets in India, cybercriminals have devised various scams to trick consumers. Common tactics include sending fake payment requests, impersonating legitimate payment apps, and conducting fraudulent transactions. These scams can lead to financial losses for unsuspecting users.

- **Online Shopping Fraud:** Indian consumers often fall victim to online shopping fraud. Scammers create fake e-commerce websites that mimic well-known platforms, enticing shoppers with unrealistically low prices. Consumers make payments but receive counterfeit or non-existent products, resulting in financial losses.

- **Telecom Phishing:** Scammers impersonate telecom service providers and contact consumers through phone calls or text messages, claiming that their SIM cards need verification or replacement. Unsuspecting individuals provide personal information or share OTPs (One-Time Passwords), enabling scammers to take over their mobile accounts or commit identity theft.

- **Job Scams:** Fraudsters advertise fake job opportunities, preying on job seekers in India. They may ask for an upfront payment for job placement, offer non-existent positions, or use deceptive tactics to collect personal information for identity theft. Job seekers can suffer financial losses and identity-related issues.

- **Lottery and Prize Scams:** Consumers in India are often targeted with fraudulent lottery or prize-winning notifications. Scammers inform victims that they've won large sums of money or valuable prizes and request fees or taxes to claim the winnings. Victims end up losing money without receiving any rewards.

These examples emphasize the importance of consumer awareness and vigilance in the digital age. Consumers should exercise caution when engaging in online transactions, verify the legitimacy of offers and requests, and stay informed about common fraud tactics to protect themselves from falling victim to scams.

The Interconnectedness of Our Digital Lives

Our lives have become increasingly interconnected in the digital realm. We store personal information in the cloud, conduct financial transactions online, and rely on interconnected systems for essential services. This interconnectedness means that the impact of a cyber incident can cascade through multiple facets of our lives, affecting not only individuals but entire communities and nations.

In conclusion, cybersecurity is not an abstract concern; it is a fundamental requirement for the preservation of our way of life in the digital age. It is about protecting our identities, our financial well-being, our trust in institutions, and our national security. The subsequent chapters of this discussion will delve into strategies for bolstering cybersecurity, from best practices for individuals to the role of governments and organizations in safeguarding our digital future.

Scope and Purpose of the Book

Against this backdrop of the digital era and the escalating threats it brings, this book emerges as a guide, an educator, and a defense mechanism. Its purpose is twofold: to empower readers with knowledge that mitigates risk and to foster a culture of cyber resilience.

The scope of this book is comprehensive, spanning the entire spectrum of cyber threats and cybersecurity measures. It delves into the world of cybercriminals and their tactics, offering insights into their motivations and methods. It uncovers the psychology behind cyber frauds, helping readers recognize red flags and stay one step ahead.

Additionally, this book equips readers with actionable strategies to protect themselves and their digital footprint. From understanding the importance of strong passwords to navigating the intricacies of encryption, every chapter is a toolkit for cyber resilience.

In essence, this book is not just a collection of chapters; it's a shield against the ever-evolving landscape of cyber threats. It's an invitation to embark on a journey of discovery, empowerment, and preparedness in the face of the digital unknown.It encapsulates the dynamic interplay between technology, threat, and resilience. It's a call to action, a resource, and a reminder that while the digital era presents boundless opportunities, it also demands our vigilance. By understanding cyber threats, embracing cybersecurity, and adopting proactive measures, we can navigate the digital landscape with wisdom and resilience.

Chapter 2

TYPES OF CYBER FRAUDS

Phishing and Spear Phishing

In the digital age, where our lives are intertwined with the virtual realm, cybercriminals have devised ingenious ways to exploit our trust and manipulate our behaviors. Among the myriad forms of cyber fraud, one tactic stands out as one of the most pervasive and damaging: phishing.

Phishing Attacks: A Closer Look

Phishing attacks are a prevalent and insidious form of cybercrime that target individuals and organizations alike. They leverage psychological manipulation, social engineering, and deception to trick victims into taking actions that benefit cybercriminals, such as revealing sensitive information, downloading malware, or making fraudulent payments. Let's delve deeper into the examples of phishing attacks mentioned:

1. The Urgent Password Update:
   - In this scenario, cybercriminals exploit fear and urgency. The victim receives an email claiming that their account has been compromised or that there has been unauthorized access.
   - The email typically includes a link that directs the victim to a fake login page designed to resemble a legitimate website. These fake pages are often meticulously crafted to look authentic.
   - Once on the fake login page, victims are prompted to enter their username and password, thinking they are securing their account.
   - However, the entered credentials are captured by the cybercriminals, who can then use them to gain unauthorized access to the victim's account, commit identity theft, or carry out further malicious activities.

2. The Fake Retail Deal:
   - This phishing attack plays on the victim's desire for a good deal or exclusive offer. The victim receives an email advertising unbelievably low prices or attractive discounts from a well-known retailer.
   - The email contains links that lead to fraudulent websites designed to mimic the legitimate online store. These fake websites may even include counterfeit logos and product listings.
   - Victims, eager to take advantage of the deal, make purchases and provide their payment details, thinking they are buying genuine products.
   - However, they soon discover that they have fallen victim to a scam, as they receive either subpar or counterfeit goods, or no products at all.

3. The Charity Scam:
   - This phishing tactic preys on the victim's empathy and desire to help during times of crisis, such as natural disasters or humanitarian emergencies.
   - Victims receive emails or messages that appear to be from charitable organizations, claiming to be raising funds for disaster relief efforts or other noble causes.
   - These emails often contain emotional appeals and heart-wrenching stories to persuade recipients to make donations.
   - Unfortunately, the funds sent to the provided details usually end up in the hands of cybercriminals, and no real charitable work is carried out.

4. The Tax Refund Ruse:
    o Cybercriminals use this tactic to exploit the victim's desire for financial gain. The victim receives an email purporting to be from a tax authority, promising a substantial tax refund.
    o To claim the refund, victims are instructed to provide personal and financial information, including bank account details.
    o The cybercriminals use this stolen information for various malicious purposes, including identity theft, fraudulent financial transactions, or selling the data on the dark web.

To protect against phishing attacks, individuals and organizations must exercise caution when receiving unsolicited emails or messages, especially those requesting sensitive information or immediate action. Verify the authenticity of the sender, double-check URLs, and avoid clicking on suspicious links or downloading attachments from unknown sources. Additionally, cybersecurity awareness and training play a crucial role in helping individuals recognize and respond to phishing attempts effectively.

Spear Phishing: The Art of Precision Targeting

Spear phishing represents a significant escalation in cybercriminal tactics compared to traditional phishing. Rather than casting a wide net in the hope of catching a few victims, spear phishing is akin to using a precision-guided missile, with cybercriminals tailoring their attacks to exploit specific individuals or organizations. This advanced form of phishing relies on the meticulous customization of email content, making it highly convincing and difficult to detect.

Here, we will delve into the nuances of spear phishing, exploring its personalized nature and various real-world scenarios:

1. The Executive Impersonation:
    o In this scenario, cybercriminals meticulously research an organization to identify high-ranking executives or individuals with financial authority.
    o They then craft emails that impersonate these executives, often using similar email addresses or mimicking the company's email format.

- o The email typically contains urgent and confidential requests, such as instructing employees to transfer funds to what appears to be a legitimate account. Since the email appears to come from a trusted source, victims may comply, resulting in significant financial losses.

2. The Job Offer:
   - o Spear phishing isn't limited to organizations; it can also target individuals seeking employment opportunities.
   - o Cybercriminals scour job search websites and social media platforms to identify job seekers.
   - o They send enticing job offers that promise high salaries, attractive benefits, and career growth.
   - o To proceed with the supposed job application, victims are asked to provide personal information, including Social Security numbers or copies of identification documents. In some cases, they may be asked to pay upfront fees for processing.

3. The Family Emergency:
   - o This emotionally manipulative spear phishing tactic preys on individuals' natural instinct to help loved ones in times of crisis.
   - o Cybercriminals pose as family members or close friends, often using compromised email accounts or stolen contact lists.
   - o They send urgent messages claiming to be in dire situations, such as accidents, arrests, or medical emergencies.
   - o Victims, driven by concern and the desire to assist, may be coerced into sending money or sensitive information, believing they are helping someone they care about.

The effectiveness of spear phishing lies in its ability to create a sense of familiarity and trust. Attackers meticulously research their targets, gathering publicly available information from social media profiles, corporate websites, and other online sources. This information is then used to craft convincing emails that reference recent activities, events, or personal relationships.

Defending Consumers Against Spear Phishing Attacks

Individuals, just like organizations, are at risk of falling victim to spear phishing attacks. To protect themselves from these targeted and deceptive threats, consumers can take the following cybersecurity measures:

1. Cybersecurity Awareness:
    o   **Stay Informed:** Consumers should stay updated on the latest cybersecurity threats, including spear phishing. Knowledge is the first line of defense against these attacks.
    o   **Recognizing Red Flags:** Educate yourself about common indicators of spear phishing, such as suspicious sender email addresses or requests for sensitive information.

2. Email Security:
    o   **Email Authentication:** Consumers can make use of email authentication protocols like DMARC to verify the authenticity of incoming emails, reducing the chances of falling for email spoofing.
    o   **Multi-Factor Authentication (MFA):** Enable MFA for email accounts and any other systems that support it. MFA adds an extra layer of security and can prevent unauthorized access.

3. Email Filtering:
    o   **Advanced Filtering Solutions:** Consider using advanced email filtering solutions that can identify and quarantining suspicious messages. These solutions can help prevent phishing emails from reaching your inbox.

4. Verification:
    o   **Alternate Verification Channels:** It's a good practice to verify any unusual or sensitive requests received via email through alternate channels, such as a phone call to the purported sender. This can help confirm the legitimacy of the request.

5. Regular Software Updates:
    o   **Keep Software Updated:** Ensure that your email client and operating system are up to date with the latest security patches. Cybercriminals often target known vulnerabilities.

6. Strong and Unique Passwords:
   o **Secure Credentials:** Use strong and unique passwords for email and online accounts. Avoid using easily guessable information like birthdays or common words.

7. Phishing Simulations:
   o **Self-Testing:** Some security tools offer phishing simulation services. Consumers can use these to test their ability to recognize phishing attempts and improve their responses.

8. Anti-Phishing Browser Extensions:
   o **Additional Protection:** Consider using browser extensions designed to detect and block phishing websites. These extensions can provide an added layer of defense against phishing attempts.

Spear phishing attacks continue to evolve, becoming increasingly sophisticated and difficult to detect. Consumers, as well as organizations, must remain vigilant and proactive in their approach to cybersecurity. By staying informed, practicing good cybersecurity hygiene, and implementing robust defense mechanisms, individuals can significantly reduce their susceptibility to these highly targeted and deceptive attacks.

Implications and Prevention

The implications of falling victim to phishing or spear phishing attacks are far-reaching. Stolen login credentials can lead to unauthorized access to sensitive accounts, financial losses, and even identity theft. Beyond individual repercussions, phishing attacks can compromise organizations by providing cybercriminals with a foothold into their systems.

Preventing phishing attacks requires a blend of awareness, vigilance, and technology. Education is paramount: users need to be trained to recognize the telltale signs of phishing emails, such as mismatched URLs, poor grammar, or unsolicited requests for sensitive information. Additionally, robust email filters and authentication mechanisms can help filter out phishing attempts, while multi-factor authentication provides an additional layer of security.

In conclusion, phishing and spear phishing are not just technical exploits; they are psychological manipulations that exploit human vulnerabilities. As the digital landscape evolves, it's imperative for individuals and organizations to fortify themselves against these fraudulent tactics. By cultivating a culture of cybersecurity awareness and adopting preventive measures, we can safeguard our digital identities and financial well-being from the clutches of cybercriminals. It is essential to remember that in the evolving world of cybercrime, staying vigilant and informed is our best defense.

Identity Theft and Digital Impersonation

In the intricate tapestry of the digital world, identity is the linchpin that connects us to various online services and platforms. Our digital identities, composed of personal information, financial details, and online interactions, hold significant value in today's interconnected society. However, this very interconnectedness has given rise to a formidable adversary: identity theft and digital impersonation.

Identity Theft: A Modern-Day Heist

Identity theft stands as a pervasive and damaging cybercrime that mirrors the audacity of a modern-day heist. In this digital age, cybercriminals execute their schemes with finesse, stealthily pilfering personal information to impersonate their victims. The repercussions of identity theft can cascade from severe financial consequences to lasting reputational damage, affecting individuals and organizations alike.

What makes identity theft particularly alarming is the wide array of methods and techniques employed by cybercriminals. They are known to infiltrate databases containing personal records, intercept unsecured communications, or cunningly employ phishing tactics to gather sensitive data. Armed with this information, these criminals can perpetrate a myriad of fraudulent activities, ranging from opening fake bank accounts to applying for loans or making unauthorized purchases. Here, we delve into some pertinent examples of identity theft and data breaches that have had a substantial and lasting impact:

Financial Fraud: Identity thieves are adept at obtaining critical financial information, including credit card details, bank account numbers, or Social Security numbers. Armed with this data, they engage in a variety of nefarious activities such as siphoning funds from bank accounts, making unauthorized purchases, or committing credit card fraud. Two significant examples are:

- **The Capital One Data Breach (2019):** In one of the largest data breaches in history, a former employee of a cloud hosting company exploited a vulnerability in Capital One's systems, compromising the data of over 100 million customers. The breach exposed not only personal information but also credit card application data, leading to significant financial and reputational damage.

- **The Experian Data Breach (2020):** Experian, one of the major credit reporting agencies, experienced a data breach that exposed personal and financial information of millions of individuals. This breach had far-reaching implications, as it involved the data of customers from several financial institutions that relied on Experian's services.

- **Medical Identity Theft:** Cybercriminals venture into the realm of medical records, aiming to obtain prescription medications, submit fraudulent insurance claims, or exploit sensitive health data. Beyond causing financial harm, medical identity theft can potentially endanger individuals' health. The Premera Blue Cross data breach in 2015 serves as a stark example:

- **The Premera Blue Cross Data Breach (2015):** In this significant healthcare data breach, hackers infiltrated the systems of Premera Blue Cross, a major health insurance provider in the Pacific Northwest. The breach exposed the personal and medical information of millions of individuals, compromising their privacy and potentially putting their health at risk.

- **Criminal Identity Theft:** A particularly harrowing facet of identity theft involves fraudsters assuming the identity of another person when engaging in criminal activities. This not only leads to wrongful accusations but also results in legal implications for the innocent victim. Instances where individuals are falsely arrested or accused due to their stolen identities underscore the gravity of this issue.

In summary, identity theft is a modern-day heist orchestrated with remarkable sophistication by cybercriminals. It highlights the vulnerability of individuals and organizations in an era of digital interconnectedness. By understanding the methods employed by these criminals and adopting robust cybersecurity measures, individuals and entities can better protect themselves from the potentially devastating consequences of identity theft. The fight against identity theft is an ongoing battle, one that requires vigilance, awareness, and a commitment to safeguarding sensitive information in the digital age.

Digital Impersonation: The Art of Deception

Digital impersonation takes identity theft a step further, weaving an intricate web of deceit through various online channels. In this age of advanced technology,

Identity Theft: A Modern-Day Heist

Identity theft stands as a pervasive and damaging cybercrime that mirrors the audacity of a modern-day heist. In this digital age, cybercriminals execute their schemes with finesse, stealthily pilfering personal information to impersonate their victims. The repercussions of identity theft can cascade from severe financial consequences to lasting reputational damage, affecting individuals and organizations alike.

What makes identity theft particularly alarming is the wide array of methods and techniques employed by cybercriminals. They are known to infiltrate databases containing personal records, intercept unsecured communications, or cunningly employ phishing tactics to gather sensitive data. Armed with this information, these criminals can perpetrate a myriad of fraudulent activities, ranging from opening fake bank accounts to applying for loans or making unauthorized purchases. Here, we delve into some pertinent examples of identity theft and data breaches that have had a substantial and lasting impact:

- **Credit Card Fraud:** A cybercriminal obtains an individual's credit card information and uses it to make unauthorized purchases or withdrawals. The victim may notice unfamiliar charges on their credit card statement.

- **Phishing Scams:** An individual receives an email or message that appears to be from a legitimate organization, asking for personal or financial information. If the person falls for the scam and provides their details, the cybercriminal can use the information for identity theft.

- **Medical Identity Theft:** An identity thief uses someone else's personal information to obtain medical treatment or prescription medications. This can lead to fraudulent insurance claims and medical records inaccuracies.

- **Tax Fraud:** Identity thieves may use stolen Social Security numbers to file fraudulent tax returns and claim refunds in the victim's name, resulting in financial losses and tax-related complications.

- **Bank Account Takeover:** Cybercriminals gain access to an individual's bank account by obtaining login credentials or personal information. They may then make unauthorized withdrawals, transfer funds, or engage in other fraudulent activities.

- **Criminal Identity Theft:** An identity thief commits a crime while assuming the identity of another person. The innocent victim may face legal consequences, including wrongful arrests or accusations.

- **Child Identity Theft:** Identity thieves may target minors, using their personal information to open fraudulent accounts or access benefits. Since children don't typically monitor their credit, such theft can go unnoticed for years.

- **Social Security Identity Theft:** An identity thief may fraudulently obtain someone's Social Security benefits, compromising the victim's financial security and government support.

- **Utility Fraud:** Identity thieves may open utility service accounts in someone else's name and leave unpaid bills, which can damage the victim's credit and result in service disruptions.
- **Online Account Hacking:** Cybercriminals may gain unauthorized access to an individual's online accounts, such as email or social media. Once inside, they can impersonate the victim or use the account for malicious activities.

Identity thieves are adept at obtaining critical financial information, including credit card details, bank account numbers, or Social Security numbers/ Aadhar and PAN numbers. Armed with this data, they engage in a variety of nefarious activities such as siphoning funds from bank accounts, making unauthorized purchases, or committing credit card fraud. Two significant examples are:

- **The Capital One Data Breach (2019):** In one of the largest data breaches in history, a former employee of a cloud hosting company exploited a vulnerability in Capital One's systems, compromising the data of over 100 million customers. The breach exposed not only personal information but also credit card application data, leading to significant financial and reputational damage.
- **The Experian Data Breach (2020):** Experian, one of the major credit reporting agencies, experienced a data breach that exposed personal and financial information of millions of individuals. This breach had far-reaching implications, as it involved the data of customers from several financial institutions that relied on Experian's services.
- **Medical Identity Theft:** Cybercriminals venture into the realm of medical records, aiming to obtain prescription medications, submit fraudulent insurance claims, or exploit sensitive health data. Beyond causing financial harm, medical identity theft can potentially endanger individuals' health. The Premera Blue Cross data breach in 2015 serves as a stark example:
- **The Premera Blue Cross Data Breach (2015):** In this significant healthcare data breach, hackers infiltrated the systems of Premera Blue Cross, a major health insurance provider in the Pacific Northwest. The breach exposed the personal and medical information of millions of individuals, compromising their privacy and potentially putting their health at risk.

In summary, identity theft is a modern-day heist orchestrated with remarkable sophistication by cybercriminals. It highlights the vulnerability of individuals and organizations in an era of digital interconnectedness. By understanding the methods employed by these criminals and adopting robust cybersecurity measures, individuals and entities can better protect themselves from the potentially devastating consequences of identity theft. The fight against identity theft is an ongoing battle, one that requires vigilance, awareness, and a commitment to safeguarding sensitive information in the digital age.

Preventing Identity Theft and Impersonation: Safeguarding Your Digital Persona

In an era where our digital lives intertwine seamlessly with our real-world identities, it's imperative to adopt a proactive approach to mitigate the risks of identity theft and digital impersonation. These cyber threats lurk in the shadows of the digital realm, waiting for vulnerabilities to exploit. Whether you're an individual seeking to protect your personal information or an organization safeguarding sensitive data, here are key strategies to fortify your defenses:

1. **Two-Factor Authentication (2FA):** The Power of Two
   - Two-Factor Authentication, or 2FA, stands as a formidable defense against identity theft. By enabling 2FA, you add an additional layer of security beyond the conventional password. This secondary verification method could be a text message code, a fingerprint scan, or a hardware token. Even if cybercriminals manage to steal your password, they would still need this secondary credential to access your account. It's akin to having a second lock on your digital door, and it significantly enhances your security.

2. **Regular Account Monitoring:** Keeping a Watchful Eye
   - Vigilance is paramount in the digital age. Regularly monitoring your financial accounts, credit reports, and online profiles can help detect unauthorized activities early. Review your bank statements diligently, scrutinize your credit reports for any unusual activity, and keep an eye on your social media profiles for signs of unauthorized access. Early detection allows you to take swift action to mitigate potential damage.

3. **Vigilance on Social Media:** Share Wisely
   - Social media platforms are treasure troves of personal information, making them prime hunting grounds for cybercriminals looking to craft convincing impersonations. To safeguard your digital identity, avoid sharing sensitive personal information publicly. Cybercriminals often exploit publicly available data, such as birthdates, hometowns, and family details, to create convincing impersonations. Be cautious about what you share and adjust your privacy settings to restrict access to sensitive information.

4. **Cybersecurity Training:** Knowledge is Defense
   - For organizations, one of the most potent weapons against identity theft and impersonation is a well-informed workforce. Conduct cybersecurity awareness training for your employees, emphasizing the dangers of phishing, impersonation attempts, and the importance of robust password practices. Educated employees are more likely to recognize and thwart cyber threats, bolstering the overall cybersecurity posture of your organization.

5. **Strong Password Practices:** Building Digital Fortresses
   - Encourage the use of strong, complex passwords across all accounts. Discourage password reuse, as this can have devastating consequences if one account is compromised. Implement password policies that require a combination of upper and lower case letters, numbers, and special characters. Consider using reputable password managers to generate and securely store complex passwords.

6. **Data Encryption:** Locking Your Digital Secrets
   - Data encryption is your digital fortress, protecting sensitive information both in transit and at rest. Utilize encryption technologies to safeguard data as it travels across networks and when it's stored on devices or servers. Encryption ensures that even if cybercriminals gain access to your data, they won't be able to decipher it without the encryption key.

7. **Secure Communication Channels:** Shielding Your Conversations
   - Encourage the use of secure communication channels for sensitive discussions. Encrypted email services and messaging platforms with

end-to-end encryption add an extra layer of privacy to your digital conversations. When sharing sensitive information or discussing confidential matters, opt for these secure channels to prevent interception and eavesdropping.

In conclusion, the digital landscape offers unparalleled convenience and connectivity, but it's also rife with threats to your digital identity. Recognizing the tactics employed by cybercriminals, adopting robust cybersecurity practices, and fostering a culture of digital awareness are essential for navigating this treacherous terrain. By safeguarding our digital identities, we can continue to reap the boundless benefits of the digital age while preserving our personal and financial integrity. Our vigilance and unwavering commitment to cybersecurity serve as the keys to staying one step ahead of digital impostors and protecting our digital selves in an ever-evolving digital landscape.

Online Scams and Confidence Tricks - Navigating the Digital Deception

In the vast and interconnected landscape of the internet, a shadowy world thrives—one inhabited by online scams and confidence tricks. These contemporary plagues rely on the manipulation of human psychology, trust, and sometimes sheer ignorance to extract personal and financial gain from unsuspecting victims. As we traverse this digital frontier, it becomes increasingly crucial to not only recognize the tactics employed by these scammers but also arm ourselves with knowledge to fend off their nefarious designs.

The Anatomy of Online Scams

Online scams are intricate, well-orchestrated schemes designed to deceive individuals into parting with their money, personal information, or both. They prey on psychological triggers, exploit vulnerabilities, and often present themselves as opportunities that are too good to be true. These scams cast a wide net, targeting a broad spectrum of victims, from tech-savvy youngsters to seasoned professionals, leaving a trail of financial ruin and emotional distress in their wake.

Advance Fee Fraud: The "Nigerian Prince" Scam

One of the classics in the world of online scams is the Advance Fee Fraud, often humorously referred to as the "Nigerian Prince" scam. In this ploy, a fraudster poses as a wealthy individual who promises the victim a substantial sum of money in exchange for a small upfront fee. Victims are lured into believing they are on the brink of receiving a windfall, only to lose their initial payment and any additional funds they provide.

Lottery and Prize Scams: Illusory Winnings

Lottery and prize scams tantalize victims with messages claiming they've won a lottery, sweepstakes, or prize draw that they never even entered. To claim their "winnings," victims are asked to pay various fees or taxes upfront. They end up losing money without ever receiving the promised prize.

Investment Schemes: Deceptive Financial Advisors

Scammers adeptly pose as financial advisors or offer enticing investment opportunities that promise high returns. Victims eagerly invest their hard-earned money, only to later discover that the entire scheme was nothing more than a ruse, and their funds have disappeared into the ether.

Romance Scams: Matters of the Heart Turn Dark

In romance scams, fraudsters take on fake identities and build emotional connections with victims through online dating platforms. Once trust is established, these scammers manipulate their victims into sending money or valuable items under the pretense of various emergency situations or travel expenses. What begins as a promising romance often ends in financial losses and emotional turmoil.

The Confidence Trick: Playing on Emotions

Confidence tricks, also known as "cons," constitute a subcategory of scams that primarily rely on psychological manipulation to deceive victims. These schemes exploit human trust, sympathy, and our innate desire to help others.

The Grandparent Scam: Preying on Love and Concern

One heart-wrenching example is the Grandparent Scam. In this scenario, scammers impersonate distressed grandchildren in urgent need of financial assistance. Driven by love and concern for their loved ones, the elderly victim wires money to the scammer, only to later discover the cruel deception.

Tech Support Scams: Exploiting Trust in Tech

Tech support scams involve fraudsters who contact victims, posing as tech support personnel from reputable companies. They claim that the victim's computer is infected or experiencing technical issues, and they offer to fix it for a fee. In reality, they are seeking access to the victim's device and sensitive information.

Psychic Scams: Promises of the Supernatural

Psychic scams involve fraudulent psychics who promise to lift curses, predict fortunes, or provide life-changing advice in exchange for exorbitant fees. Victims end up paying for empty promises and fabricated services, driven by their hope for a better future.

Utility Scams: Threats and Coercion

Utility scams involve impostors pretending to represent utility companies. They threaten to cut off essential services, such as electricity or water, unless immediate payment is made. Victims, fearing the consequences of a service cutoff, are coerced into paying the fraudulent charge.

Defending Against Online Scams and Cons

Preventing falling prey to online scams and confidence tricks requires a combination of awareness, skepticism, and caution. By understanding common tactics and adopting vigilant behaviors, individuals can fortify themselves against these insidious threats.

1. **Question Everything:** Skepticism as a Shield
   - Practice healthy skepticism when encountering unsolicited messages, offers that sound too good to be true, and high-pressure sales tactics. Always verify the legitimacy of the source independently before taking any action.

2. **Stay Informed:** Knowledge is Armor
   - Stay informed about the latest scams and tricks circulating online. Awareness is your first line of defense. Regularly research and educate yourself about common scams and the tactics used by scammers.

3. **Secure Personal Information:** Guard Your Data
   - Exercise caution when sharing personal or financial information online, especially with unknown individuals or entities. Be mindful of the information you make public on social media and other platforms, as cybercriminals often exploit publicly available data for impersonation.

4. **Two-Factor Authentication:** Double Lock Your Digital Door
   - Enable Two-Factor Authentication (2FA) wherever it is offered. This additional layer of security can significantly reduce the risk of unauthorized access to your accounts.

5. **Check URLs:** Verify the Web
   - Before providing sensitive information online, ensure the legitimacy of websites. Look for "https://" in the URL, which indicates a secure connection, and make sure the website's spelling is correct. Double-check the source to avoid phishing sites.

6. **Report Suspicious Activity:** Be a Digital Vigilante
   - If you suspect you've encountered a scam or confidence trick, report it to the appropriate authorities or platforms. Your action may prevent others from falling victim to the same scheme.

In conclusion, online scams and confidence tricks are virtual embodiments of age-old cons, reinvented for the digital era.

Social Engineering and Manipulation

In the vast expanse of cyberspace, where virtual connections bridge the gaps between individuals and organizations, a more insidious form of deception thrives: social engineering. This crafty art of manipulation preys not on technology vulnerabilities, but on the very human characteristics that define us—trust, empathy, and curiosity. Unveiling the tactics and examples of social engineering is crucial in protecting ourselves from these psychological traps.

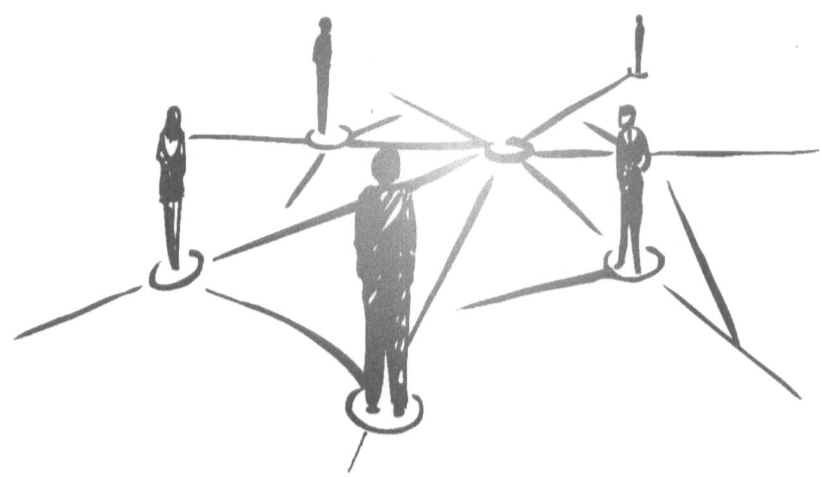

Understanding Social Engineering: A Technical Perspective

Social engineering, from a technical standpoint, is a form of psychological manipulation where attackers exploit human psychology, trust, and cognitive biases to gain unauthorized access to systems, steal sensitive information, or manipulate victims into performing actions against their own interests. Let's delve into the technical aspects of various social engineering tactics with real-world examples.

Phishing for Information

- Pretexting: Attackers may impersonate trusted entities through emails, calls, or even in-person encounters. For example, a cybercriminal might send an email appearing to be from a bank, requesting users to verify their account information by clicking on a link that leads to a fake website.

The victim, thinking it's legitimate, provides sensitive data, which the attacker later exploits.

○ Example: The 2016 email phishing campaign targeting Gmail users used a deceptive link that closely resembled a Google sign-in page. Victims who entered their credentials unknowingly gave access to their accounts.

• Tailgating: In physical social engineering scenarios, attackers exploit human courtesy or lack of awareness. A classic example is when an attacker follows an employee into a secure facility by holding the door open, without needing to bypass electronic security measures.

○ Example: In 2007, undercover reporters from the TV show "Dateline NBC" demonstrated tailgating by infiltrating multiple U.S. government buildings.

• Impersonation: Technical aspects of impersonation involve creating convincing fake profiles on social media. Attackers often gather personal details from public sources to make their impersonation believable. They may use these profiles to initiate contact, gain trust, and exploit victims.

○ Example: The "Jayson Blair" catfishing case involved the creation of a fake online identity by a journalist, who impersonated a firefighter to gain the trust of his victims and solicit donations for fabricated causes.

• Baiting: Cybercriminals place infected media devices in public spaces. If someone picks up the device and connects it to their computer, malware is automatically executed, compromising the victim's system.

○ Example: In 2008, USB sticks were scattered in the parking lot of a U.S. military base in the Middle East, containing malware that infected the computers of those who plugged them in.

Manipulation of Trust and Authority

• **Authority Exploitation:** Attackers may engage in email spoofing to make their messages seem to come from authoritative figures. For instance, they might impersonate the CEO of a company, instructing an employee to transfer funds to a fraudulent account.

- Example: In 2016, a cybercriminal impersonated the CEO of an Austrian aerospace manufacturer and tricked an employee into transferring 50 million euros to a fraudulent account.

- **Tech Support Scams:** Attackers impersonate tech support personnel, often through cold-calls or pop-up messages claiming malware infections. They gain remote access to victims' computers, sometimes using legitimate remote administration tools.
  - Example: The "Windows Technical Support" scam has victimized countless individuals. Fraudsters claim to be Microsoft tech support and manipulate victims into granting remote access, subsequently compromising their systems.

- **CEO Fraud:** Attackers may use email spoofing to impersonate high-level executives. They craft convincing emails that bypass spam filters and instruct employees to make unauthorized financial transactions.
  - Example: In 2019, a Belgian branch of a French company fell victim to CEO fraud when cybercriminals impersonated the company's CEO and tricked employees into transferring 6.6 million euros to a fraudulent account.

Manipulating Emotions

- **Guilt Tripping:** Attackers employ emotional manipulation through emails or calls. They craft messages designed to evoke guilt or fear, compelling victims to take actions they normally wouldn't.
  - Example: In various "fake kidnapping" scams, fraudsters impersonate kidnappers and demand ransom payments, preying on victims' fears for their loved ones' safety.

- **Urgency:** Attackers create a sense of urgency through time-sensitive threats. They may manipulate timestamps on emails or employ countdown timers to pressure victims into making quick decisions.
  - Example: Numerous phishing emails employ urgency tactics, such as claiming an account will be locked unless immediate action is taken.

- **Appealing to Empathy:** Crafting believable stories or personas requires attackers to gather intelligence on their victims. They scour social media profiles, forums, or other online sources for personal details to create convincing narratives.
  - ○ **Example:** Romance scams, where cybercriminals build emotional connections with victims before exploiting their trust, are common examples of appealing to empathy.

Social engineering and manipulation in the digital realm represent a complex interplay between psychological tactics and technical execution. Understanding these tactics, both from a psychological and technical perspective, is crucial in defending against digital deception.

Sources

Google Online Security Blog, "A new Google Docs phishing scam is sweeping the internet," May 2017.

NBC News, "Undercover Investigation: 'Tailgating' into Government Buildings," 2007.

The New York Times, "Journalist Who Faked Articles Is Reindicted," 2003.

Wired, "USB Sticks Infected with Malware Left in Parking Lot," 2008.

BBC News, "FACC, the Chinese hackers, and the $50m swindle," 2016.

Microsoft, "Avoiding tech support phone scams," 2021.

Federal Trade Commission, "Tech Support Scams," 2021.

BBC News, "Belgium bank heist: 60 arrested after fake police car used," 2019.

ABC News, "Scam used fake kidnappings to extort money from victims," 2019.

Federal Trade Commission, "Scammers Impersonate FTC," 2021.

Federal Trade Commission, "Fake 'Government Grant' Phone Scammers," 2010-2021.

Online Shopping and Auction Fraud: Technical Considerations

The allure of online shopping and the convenience of e-commerce have reshaped the way we acquire goods and services. However, with the expansion of online marketplaces comes an increase in online shopping and auction fraud. In this chapter, we delve into the tactics employed by cybercriminals to exploit unsuspecting consumers and how to guard against their schemes, including technical aspects to consider.

The E-Commerce Landscape

The digital marketplace offers an abundance of products and services, accessible from the comfort of our screens. This convenience, however, has also given rise to fraudulent activities that prey on the unwary consumer.

Types of Online Shopping Fraud

- **Fake Online Stores:** Scammers create authentic-looking websites offering products at unrealistically low prices. Unsuspecting shoppers make payments but never receive the goods. From a technical perspective, these fake stores often use deceptive web design and counterfeit security logos to appear legitimate.

- **Technical Consideration:** Fake online stores may employ domain names that closely resemble legitimate ones, use SSL certificates to appear secure, and use convincing images of products. They exploit e-commerce platforms and web hosting services to set up their fraudulent sites.
- **Phantom Goods:** Fraudsters list items for sale but never intend to deliver them. Victims pay upfront, only to be left empty-handed. Technical elements include fraudulent payment gateways that collect payments without fulfilling orders.
- **Technical Consideration:** Cybercriminals may set up fake payment processing systems that mimic legitimate ones, collecting payment information from victims. They also employ tactics to obfuscate their real identities, making it challenging for authorities to trace them.
- **Counterfeit Merchandise:** Criminals sell counterfeit or imitation products, which appear genuine but are of inferior quality or entirely different items. Technical measures may involve sophisticated counterfeit packaging and convincing product images.
- **Technical Consideration:** Creating convincing counterfeit merchandise requires expertise in manufacturing and packaging. Cybercriminals may leverage advanced printing and labeling technologies to produce convincing replicas. They often use legitimate e-commerce platforms to list these products.
- **Triangulation Fraud:** Cybercriminals use legitimate online stores to advertise products they don't possess. They then purchase the genuine product from the legitimate store and have it shipped to the victim, who pays the scammer. This involves technical manipulation of online listings and order processing.
- **Technical Consideration:** Scammers exploit vulnerabilities in legitimate e-commerce websites to manipulate product listings. They may automate the purchase process to minimize their involvement and use various payment methods to avoid detection.

Auction Fraud

- **Bid Manipulation:** Fraudsters artificially inflate the bids on auction items to create a sense of competition and drive up the price. This may involve the use of multiple fake accounts to bid on their own items, technically known as shill bidding.

- **Technical Consideration:** Bid manipulation often requires the use of proxy servers, VPNs, or anonymization techniques to conceal the fraudsters' identity. They may also employ scripting or automated tools to place bids automatically.

- **Non-Delivery of Goods:** Buyers pay for items they've won but never receive them, as the seller simply disappears. This could involve creating fake seller accounts or using temporary email addresses to avoid detection.

- **Technical Consideration:** Scammers may use disposable email addresses or compromised email accounts to communicate with victims, making it harder to trace them. They might use false registration information when creating seller accounts.

- **Misrepresentation:** Sellers falsely advertise products to attract bidders, often using images or descriptions that don't accurately represent the item. Technical elements include manipulating image metadata and crafting deceptive product descriptions.

- **Technical Consideration:** Misrepresentation may involve editing image metadata to provide false details about the product's origin or authenticity. Scammers may also use photo editing software to enhance or alter images to make them appear more appealing than the actual product.

Guarding Against Online Shopping and Auction Fraud: Technical Measures

1. **Verify the Seller:** Conduct domain and website checks to ensure the seller is legitimate. Look for SSL certificates (HTTPS) and domain age.

2. **Secure Payment:** Use secure payment methods that offer buyer protection, such as credit cards or payment platforms like PayPal. Monitor your financial statements for any unauthorized transactions.

3. **Research the Product:** Utilize online resources and product review platforms to verify the authenticity and quality of the product.
4. **Beware of Too-Good-To-Be-True Deals:** Use online tools to compare prices across different sellers to identify suspiciously low prices.
5. **Check for HTTPS:** Ensure the website uses HTTPS encryption to protect your payment and personal information. Look for security seals and trustmarks.
6. **Use Reputable Platforms:** Stick to well-known and reputable online marketplaces and auction sites with strong security measures and fraud prevention mechanisms.

Real-Life Examples

*   **The Vanishing Seller:** A buyer wins an online auction for a coveted item, pays the amount promptly, but never receives the product. The seller disappears, and the buyer is left with a financial loss.
*   **Counterfeit Tech:** A consumer buys a high-end gadget at a fraction of the price from an online store. The product arrives but turns out to be a poor-quality counterfeit.
*   **Inflated Bidding:** A bidder wins an online auction for a collectible item, only to find that the winning bid was artificially inflated by the seller's shill accounts.
*   **Phantom Tickets:** A fan purchases concert tickets from an unauthorized website, believing they're genuine. On the day of the event, the tickets are rejected at the entrance.

The world of online shopping and auction fraud is fraught with risks that can lead to financial losses and disappointment. Being informed and vigilant is key to protecting oneself from falling victim to these scams. As the digital marketplace continues to evolve, consumers must arm themselves with knowledge, cautious decision-making, and technical awareness to navigate the e-commerce landscape safely and securely. Incorporating technical scrutiny into online transactions is essential in an era where cybercriminals continuously adapt their tactics to deceive consumers.

Investment and Financial Frauds

The pursuit of financial gain has been a driving force in human behavior for centuries. However, in the digital age, this pursuit has been exploited by cybercriminals who use investment and financial frauds to deceive individuals and organizations. This chapter explores the various forms of these fraudulent activities, shedding light on their tactics and providing insights into safeguarding one's financial interests.

The Temptation of Easy Wealth

Investment and financial frauds capitalize on the desire for quick profits, promising lucrative returns with minimal effort. These scams prey on both individual investors seeking growth and organizations aiming to maximize their funds.

Types of Investment and Financial Frauds

Financial frauds have taken on various forms over the years, each designed to exploit the desire for wealth, quick returns, and financial security. In this chapter, we'll dive into the nuances of different types of investment and financial frauds, shedding light on their tactics and consequences.

1. Ponzi Schemes
   - **Overview:** Ponzi schemes are among the most notorious and enduring forms of financial fraud. Named after Charles Ponzi, who orchestrated one of the earliest recorded Ponzi schemes in the 1920s, these scams promise investors high returns with minimal risk.
   - **Tactics:** Ponzi scheme operators attract victims by offering returns that are significantly higher than those available through traditional investments. They often claim to have discovered exclusive opportunities or possess a secret formula for guaranteed profits. To create an illusion of legitimacy, early investors may receive the promised returns, encouraging them to reinvest and refer others.
   - **How It Works:** Ponzi schemes use funds from new investors to pay returns to earlier investors, creating the appearance of a successful investment. This cycle continues as long as there is a steady influx of new capital. However, when new investments slow down or investors

attempt to withdraw their funds en masse, the scheme collapses, and the majority of participants lose their investments.

- o **Consequences:** Ponzi schemes can cause substantial financial losses for victims. While early investors may receive returns, later investors often bear the brunt of the losses. Moreover, these schemes can have far-reaching economic consequences, eroding trust in financial markets and regulatory institutions.

2. Pyramid Schemes
   - o **Overview:** Pyramid schemes share some similarities with Ponzi schemes but have distinct characteristics. They rely on a hierarchical structure where participants recruit others into the scheme, promising them financial rewards based on recruitment efforts rather than actual product sales or investments.
   - o **Tactics:** Pyramid schemes appeal to participants' aspirations for wealth and success. They often use persuasive marketing strategies that emphasize the potential to earn substantial income by recruiting new members. Participants are encouraged to buy into the scheme, invest money, and then recruit others to do the same.
   - o **How It Works:** In a pyramid scheme, each participant recruits new members, forming the base of the pyramid. These recruits are then expected to bring in additional members, and the process continues. Participants at the top of the pyramid benefit the most, as they receive a portion of the investments made by those lower in the hierarchy. As the pyramid expands, it becomes unsustainable, and most participants lose their investments.
   - o **Consequences:** Pyramid schemes are inherently fraudulent, and their success depends on a continuous influx of new recruits. As the scheme grows, the number of potential recruits dwindles, leading to financial losses for the majority of participants. Pyramid schemes often collapse rapidly, leaving many individuals with nothing to show for their investments.

3. Advance Fee Frauds
   - o **Overview:** Advance fee frauds are characterized by scammers who request an upfront payment or fee from victims in exchange for a promised investment opportunity, loan, or financial windfall.

- o **Tactics:** Scammers exploit victims' desire for financial gain by presenting them with enticing opportunities that seem too good to pass up. These opportunities may include investment deals, business loans, or inheritance claims. To proceed, victims are asked to make an upfront payment to cover alleged fees, taxes, or administrative costs.
- o **How It Works:** Once the victim makes the upfront payment, the scammer often disappears, and the promised investment or opportunity never materializes. Victims are left with financial losses and no recourse for recovering their funds.
- o **Consequences:** Advance fee frauds can result in significant financial harm to victims who lose not only the upfront payment but also the anticipated returns from the promised opportunity. These scams prey on victims' trust and eagerness to secure financial advantages.

4. Insider Trading
   - o **Overview:** Insider trading is a form of investment fraud that involves individuals using non-public, confidential information to buy or sell stocks or other securities, giving them an unfair advantage in the financial markets.
   - o **Tactics:** Insider traders typically have access to material, non-public information about a company's financial performance, business prospects, or upcoming events. They use this privileged information to make informed investment decisions before the information becomes available to the public.
   - o **How It Works:** Insider trading can involve buying securities when insiders expect the price to rise or selling when they expect it to fall based on undisclosed information. This activity undermines the integrity of financial markets, as it creates an uneven playing field where insiders profit at the expense of other investors who lack access to the same information.
   - o **Consequences:** Insider trading is illegal in most jurisdictions and can result in severe legal penalties, including fines and imprisonment. Moreover, it erodes trust in financial markets and can lead to financial losses for unsuspecting investors who are not privy to insider information.

Guarding Against Investment and Financial Frauds

Protecting oneself from investment and financial frauds requires a combination of vigilance, skepticism, and informed decision-making. Here are essential strategies to guard against falling victim to these scams:

- **Due Diligence:** Thoroughly research any investment opportunity before committing funds. This includes verifying the legitimacy of the investment firm, checking its regulatory status, and understanding the terms and associated risks. Reputable investments should be registered with relevant regulatory authorities.
  - o **Source:** Securities and Exchange Commission (SEC), Financial Industry Regulatory Authority (FINRA), or equivalent regulatory bodies in your region.

- **Too-Good-To-Be-True Offers:** Be wary of investment opportunities that promise exceptionally high returns with minimal or no risk. Such offers often serve as red flags for potential scams. Remember the age-old adage: "If it sounds too good to be true, it probably is."
  - o **Source:** Investor protection and education resources provided by government agencies and financial watchdogs.

- **Independent Advice:** Seek guidance from qualified financial professionals who have no association with the investment opportunity or firm in question. Independent advisors can provide unbiased insights and help you assess the legitimacy and suitability of an investment.
  - o **Source:** Certified financial planners, registered investment advisors, or reputable financial institutions.

- **Investor Education:** Take the time to educate yourself about various investment vehicles, financial markets, and common investment scams. Understanding the risks and characteristics of different investments will empower you to make informed decisions.
  - o **Source:** Educational materials and courses offered by financial institutions, universities, and government agencies. Additionally, publications by trusted financial experts and books on investment literacy.

- **Secure Communication:** Be cautious when receiving unsolicited investment offers via email, phone calls, or social media. Scammers often use these channels to reach potential victims. Verify the identity of the person or firm contacting you and refrain from sharing personal or financial information unless you are certain of their legitimacy.
  - ○ **Source:** Cybersecurity and fraud prevention guidelines provided by government agencies and reputable financial institutions.

Real-Life Examples

Understanding the consequences of investment and financial frauds through real-life examples reinforces the importance of vigilance and due diligence:

- **Bernie Madoff's Ponzi Scheme:** Bernard Madoff orchestrated one of the most notorious Ponzi schemes in history. Promising consistent high returns, Madoff lured investors into his scheme, which eventually collapsed in 2008. Thousands of investors lost an estimated $64.8 billion.
  - ○ **Source:** Court documents, SEC reports, and investigative journalism.

- **Enron Scandal:** Enron Corporation, once a respected energy company, engaged in widespread accounting fraud to artificially inflate profits. The scandal came to light in 2001, leading to Enron's bankruptcy, the loss of thousands of jobs, and significant financial losses for investors.
  - ○ **Source:** Official reports, congressional hearings, and documentaries.

- **Charles Ponzi:** Charles Ponzi, the namesake of Ponzi schemes, famously convinced investors to purchase international reply coupons at a discount, promising substantial returns within a short period. However, Ponzi used funds from new investors to pay earlier ones, leading to the scheme's collapse.
  - ○ **Source:** Historical accounts and investigations into Ponzi's fraudulent activities.

- **Affinity Fraud:** In affinity fraud cases, fraudsters exploit trust within specific groups, such as religious or ethnic communities. Promising insider investment opportunities, these scammers manipulate group members into investing, resulting in substantial losses.
  - ○ **Source:** Legal cases and reports on affinity fraud investigations.

Guarding against investment and financial frauds requires a combination of caution, research, and education. Learning from real-life examples serves as a stark reminder of the devastating consequences these scams can have on individuals and communities. By following best practices and staying informed, individuals can protect their financial interests and contribute to a safer investment landscape. As the financial landscape evolves, staying informed and cautious is essential to navigate the complex world of investments and protect one's hard-earned funds from falling into the hands of fraudsters.

Malware Attacks: Viruses, Trojans, and Ransomware: A Technical Perspective

In the realm of cyber threats, malicious software, commonly known as malware, stands as a potent weapon wielded by cybercriminals to compromise digital devices, steal sensitive information, and wreak havoc. This chapter delves into the various forms of malware attacks, shedding light on their destructive capabilities and providing insights into protecting oneself from their insidious grasp, including the technical intricacies involved.

- **Malware:** The Silent Invaders
  - o Malware is a broad term encompassing a variety of software designed to infiltrate, damage, or gain unauthorized access to computer systems. These programs exploit vulnerabilities in software, hardware, or human behavior to carry out their nefarious objectives.

Types of Malware Attacks

- **Viruses:** These programs attach themselves to legitimate files, replicating and spreading when the infected file is executed. They can corrupt or delete data and affect system performance. Viruses often use complex infection mechanisms to evade detection by antivirus software. They may employ polymorphic techniques, which change their code every time they infect a new host, making signature-based detection challenging.

- **Trojans:** Named after the legendary wooden horse, Trojans appear harmless but harbor malicious intent. Once installed, they can provide unauthorized access to attackers, steal sensitive information, or execute malicious activities. Trojans are often distributed through social engineering, tricking users into running them. Attackers may use rootkit techniques to hide their presence on infected systems, making them difficult to detect.

- **Ransomware:** This category of malware encrypts a victim's files or entire system, rendering them inaccessible. Attackers demand a ransom payment in exchange for the decryption key. Ransomware often employs advanced encryption algorithms, making decryption without the key virtually impossible. Technical defenses involve regular data backups and security measures to prevent initial infection.

- **Keyloggers:** These programs track and record keystrokes, capturing sensitive information like passwords and credit card details, which are then sent to the attacker. Keyloggers can use various evasion techniques, including rootkit functionality and encryption for exfiltrated data.

- **Botnets:** A network of infected devices, botnets are controlled by a single entity to carry out coordinated attacks, such as Distributed Denial of Service (DDoS) attacks. Botnets rely on techniques like fast-flux DNS to constantly change the IP addresses of infected hosts, making it difficult to locate and shut down command and control servers.

Protecting Against Malware Attacks: Technical Measures

1. **Regular Software Updates:** Keep operating systems, applications, and antivirus software up to date to mitigate vulnerabilities. Employ vulnerability scanning tools to identify and patch weaknesses.
2. **Secure Downloads:** Download software only from official sources and use application whitelisting to restrict unauthorized software execution.
3. **Email Vigilance:** Implement email filtering solutions that detect and quarantine phishing emails. Conduct regular security awareness training to educate users about the dangers of clicking on suspicious links or downloading attachments.
4. **Firewalls and Intrusion Detection Systems (IDS):** Enable firewalls to block unauthorized access to your computer. Use IDS to monitor network traffic for suspicious patterns and behaviors.
5. **Advanced Threat Detection:** Deploy advanced threat detection solutions that use behavior-based analysis and machine learning to identify and block malware.

Real-Life Examples

1. **WannaCry Ransomware:** In 2017, WannaCry infected hundreds of thousands of computers worldwide. It encrypted victims' files using the AES encryption algorithm and demanded ransom payments in Bitcoin for decryption.
2. **Stuxnet Worm:** Designed to target industrial control systems, Stuxnet worm sabotaged Iran's nuclear program by destroying uranium enrichment centrifuges. It used multiple zero-day vulnerabilities to propagate.
3. **Zeus Trojan:** Zeus targeted banking information, capturing login credentials and personal data. It employed advanced injection techniques to steal data from web forms and infected millions of computers worldwide.
4. **Melissa Virus:** In 1999, the Melissa virus spread via infected Word document attachments, causing email systems to slow down or crash. It used a macro script to replicate and spread.

Malware attacks continue to evolve, exploiting new vulnerabilities and creating new attack vectors. As technology advances, so do the capabilities of cybercriminals. Vigilance, regular updates, and awareness, combined with advanced technical defenses, remain key to protecting oneself from the pervasive threats posed by malware.

Chapter 3

UNVEILING THE TECHNIQUES

How Cybercriminals Operate

In the digital age, cybercriminals have evolved and adapted to exploit the vulnerabilities of individuals, businesses, and organizations. Understanding how cybercriminals operate is crucial for recognizing their tactics and enhancing cybersecurity measures. This chapter explores the intricacies of cybercriminal operations, shedding light on their strategies and tactics that leverage human psychology, technical vulnerabilities, and the digital ecosystem.

Understanding the Mind of a Cybercriminal

Cybercriminals are opportunistic and resourceful individuals or groups who employ a wide range of techniques to achieve their illicit objectives. Their methods can vary widely, ranging from exploiting human behavior to manipulating software vulnerabilities. To understand their operations, it's essential to delve into the mindset of a cybercriminal:

- **Profit-Driven:** Many cybercriminals are motivated by financial gain. They seek to steal sensitive information, such as credit card details, login credentials, or personal data, which they can monetize through various means, including selling on the dark web, committing financial fraud, or demanding ransoms.

- **Sophistication:** Cybercriminals often display a high level of technical expertise. They can develop or acquire sophisticated tools, such as malware or exploit kits, to facilitate their attacks. This technical proficiency enables them to target specific vulnerabilities effectively.

- **Adaptability:** Cybercriminals continuously adapt to changes in technology and security measures. As security defenses improve, cybercriminals find new techniques and vulnerabilities to exploit. They may also use evasion tactics to avoid detection by security software.

Stages of Cybercriminal Operations

Cybercriminal operations follow a series of stages, each with its specific objectives and tactics:

- **Reconnaissance:** In this initial stage, cybercriminals gather information about their target. This includes identifying potential vulnerabilities, weak points in security, and information about the target's digital infrastructure. Reconnaissance often involves open-source intelligence gathering, scanning for publicly available information on websites, social media, or other sources.

- **Weaponization:** After collecting intelligence, cybercriminals develop or acquire the necessary tools and malware to execute their attack. This may involve crafting custom malware or using off-the-shelf exploit kits.

- **Delivery:** Cybercriminals deliver their attack to the target. This can occur through various means, including phishing emails, malicious attachments, infected websites, or deceptive downloads. Social engineering tactics play a crucial role in convincing victims to interact with the delivery method.

- **Exploitation:** Once the attack is delivered, cybercriminals seek to exploit vulnerabilities within the target's system or network. Vulnerabilities may include unpatched software, misconfigurations, or weaknesses in security protocols.

- **Installation:** After gaining initial access, cybercriminals install malicious software, often referred to as "malware," on the victim's system. This malware serves as a persistent foothold, allowing them to maintain access and control over the compromised system.

- **Command and Control (C2):** Cybercriminals establish communication channels to control the compromised systems remotely. This includes sending commands to the malware, exfiltrating stolen data, and receiving updates on the compromised system's status.

- **Actions on Objectives:** With control established, cybercriminals execute their primary objectives. These objectives can vary widely, from stealing sensitive data and perpetrating financial fraud to launching further attacks or demanding ransoms from the victim.

Understanding these stages of cybercriminal operations is essential for cybersecurity professionals and individuals alike. It highlights the need for proactive cybersecurity measures, including robust threat detection, regular software updates, employee training in recognizing phishing attempts, and the implementation of strong security protocols to mitigate potential threats at each stage of an attack.

Exploiting Human Psychology in Frauds

In the world of cybercrime, understanding the intricacies of human psychology is the key to successful manipulation. Cybercriminals exploit a wide range of cognitive biases, emotional triggers, and innate tendencies to orchestrate convincing scams. Let's delve deeper into these techniques and explore additional points in psychology-based frauds:

Understanding Human Vulnerabilities

Human decision-making processes are not infallible; they are influenced by a multitude of biases and psychological tendencies. Cybercriminals are acutely aware of these vulnerabilities and leverage them to their advantage. Here are some key aspects of human psychology that cybercriminals exploit:

- **Loss Aversion:** People tend to fear losses more than they value equivalent gains. Cybercriminals use this fear to create urgency and push individuals into hasty decisions to avoid perceived losses.
- **Confirmation Bias:** Individuals seek information that confirms their existing beliefs. Fraudsters use this bias by tailoring their messages to align with the victim's preconceived notions, making their scams appear more convincing.
- **Curiosity:** Humans are naturally curious beings. Cybercriminals exploit this curiosity by using intriguing or sensational headlines in phishing emails or clickbait, leading individuals to click on malicious links or open infected attachments.
- **Reciprocity:** People feel compelled to reciprocate when they receive something for free. Cybercriminals often offer seemingly free items or services to build trust and later exploit this reciprocity to extract personal or financial information.

- **Overconfidence:** Many individuals overestimate their ability to spot scams or believe they are immune to falling victim. Cybercriminals prey on this overconfidence by presenting scams that appear too sophisticated to be fraudulent.

Common Techniques in Psychology-Based Frauds

- **Fear of Missing Out (FOMO):** This is a powerful psychological trigger that cybercriminals employ by creating a sense of urgency. They may claim that a limited-time opportunity is about to expire or suggest that others are taking advantage of the offer. This taps into individuals' fear of missing out on a valuable opportunity.
- **Authority Exploitation:** In addition to trust, people also tend to obey authority figures. Cybercriminals pose as authoritative entities, such as government agencies or well-known brands, to gain victims' compliance. They might threaten legal action or claim to have detected security issues, coercing individuals into complying with their demands.
- **Social Engineering through Social Media:** Cybercriminals mine social media platforms for personal information. They craft messages or phishing attempts that reference a victim's recent activities, hobbies, or connections, making their fraudulent communications appear more genuine.
- **Appealing to Altruism:** Some scams exploit individuals' desire to help others. Cybercriminals create fictitious charitable causes or claim to be in dire need, tugging at victims' heartstrings and convincing them to part with their money.
- **Technical Jargon and Complexity:** By inundating victims with technical jargon or complex-sounding explanations, cybercriminals create an illusion of expertise. This can make individuals feel overwhelmed or inferior, leading them to comply with the fraudster's instructions.

Recognizing these tactics and being aware of psychological vulnerabilities is crucial in guarding against frauds. It's essential for individuals and organizations to promote digital literacy, critical thinking, and cybersecurity awareness to resist these manipulative techniques effectively. Additionally, reporting suspicious activity and seeking guidance from trusted sources can help thwart the efforts of cybercriminals who exploit human psychology in their fraudulent activities.

Examples of Psychology-Based Frauds: A Closer Look

1. **Phishing Scams:** Phishing emails often use a combination of fear and curiosity to trick recipients. They may claim that the recipient's account has been compromised, urging immediate action to secure it. This fear of unauthorized access can prompt individuals to click on malicious links or provide sensitive information.

2. **Tech Support Scams:** These scams exploit individuals' trust in technology and the fear of technical issues. Victims receive unsolicited calls or pop-up messages claiming that their computer is infected or compromised. The fraudsters pose as tech support personnel and guide victims into granting remote access to their systems or paying for unnecessary services.

3. **Tax Scams:** Tax season can be a vulnerable time for many individuals. Scammers send urgent messages or make phone calls pretending to be from tax authorities, threatening legal action or claiming that the victim owes back taxes. Fear of legal repercussions or desire to resolve the issue swiftly can lead to financial losses.

4. **Online Auction and Shopping Scams:** These scams exploit the anticipation and excitement of receiving a purchased item. Victims may buy products online but receive counterfeit or inferior items. The fear of losing money or not getting the desired product can prevent victims from seeking refunds or reporting the fraud.

5. **Psychic Scams:** Fraudulent psychics appeal to individuals' curiosity about the future and desire for guidance. Victims pay significant amounts for supposed psychic services, including curse removal or fortune-telling, only to receive vague or fabricated information.

Additional Countermeasures Against Psychology-Based Frauds

- **Encourage Critical Thinking:** Promote a culture of skepticism, where individuals question unsolicited offers, requests, or alarming messages.

Encourage them to seek a second opinion or consult with trusted friends or family before taking action.

- **Reporting Mechanisms:** Establish clear reporting procedures for suspicious emails, calls, or messages. Encourage individuals to report incidents to relevant authorities or cybersecurity teams within organizations. Reporting can help track and combat fraudsters.
- **Multi-Factor Authentication (MFA):** Encourage the use of MFA for email accounts, financial accounts, and other sensitive platforms. MFA adds an extra layer of security, making it harder for cybercriminals to gain unauthorized access.
- **Continuous Education:** Regularly update individuals and employees about evolving fraud tactics. Provide real-world examples and case studies to illustrate the dangers of psychology-based scams. Knowledge is a powerful defense.
- **Community Awareness:** Foster a sense of community awareness, where individuals look out for one another. Encourage sharing of information about potential scams or frauds within social circles to protect vulnerable members.

Psychology-based frauds are built on the manipulation of human emotions, biases, and cognitive tendencies. Recognizing these tactics, staying informed, and promoting a culture of skepticism are essential in guarding against falling victim to these schemes. By equipping individuals with the knowledge and tools to counteract psychological manipulation, we can collectively reduce the success rate of these frauds and create a safer digital environment.

Deceptive Websites and Fake URLs: Unmasking Digital Camouflage - A Technical Examination

The internet has revolutionized how we access information, connect with others, and conduct transactions. However, this virtual world is not immune to deception. Deceptive websites and fake URLs are clever tools used by cybercriminals to dupe unsuspecting users and steal sensitive information. This chapter delves into the world of digital camouflage and provides a technical perspective on how individuals can spot and protect themselves from these malicious traps.

Understanding Deceptive Websites: A Technical Insight

Deceptive websites are engineered with a level of sophistication that enables them to appear legitimate, making them challenging to distinguish from authentic ones. Understanding the technical elements of deceptive websites is crucial for users to enhance their ability to detect and protect themselves from online threats. Here, we delve deeper into the technical aspects and characteristics associated with deceptive websites:

1. URL Manipulation Techniques:
    o   **Character Substitution:** Cybercriminals often employ characters that visually resemble legitimate ones within URLs. For instance, they might use "rn" instead of "m" or "1" instead of "l" to create deceptive domain names.
    o   **Similar-Looking Domains:** Deceptive websites frequently use domain names that closely mimic those of well-known and trusted sites. This strategy can involve adding hyphens, extra letters, or subdomains that resemble the original domain.

- o **URL Shorteners:** Attackers use URL shortening services to obscure the true destination of a link. This practice makes it challenging for users to discern whether a link leads to a legitimate or deceptive site.

2. Sophisticated Design Elements:
   - o **Replication of Aesthetics:** Deceptive websites meticulously replicate the visual elements of genuine websites. This includes copying fonts, color schemes, logos, and page layouts to create a convincing facade of legitimacy.
   - o **Responsive Design:** Cybercriminals often ensure that their deceptive websites are responsive, adapting to different screen sizes and devices. This level of detail adds to the illusion of authenticity.
   - o **Mobile Optimization:** Deceptive sites may be optimized for mobile browsing, catering to a wide range of users and devices.

3. Phishing Pages and Data Collection:
   - o **Imitation of Genuine Forms:** Deceptive websites often host HTML forms that mimic those found on legitimate sites, such as login or payment forms. Users are lured into entering sensitive information, which is then captured by the attackers.
   - o **JavaScript-Based Data Exfiltration:** JavaScript is frequently employed to manipulate webpages dynamically while covertly transmitting user input, such as login credentials and credit card details, to the attacker's server. This enables attackers to maintain the appearance of legitimacy while stealing data.

Spotting Deceptive Websites: Technical Analysis

Users can employ technical analysis to identify and protect themselves from deceptive websites more effectively:

1. URL Inspection:
   - o **Check for Character Substitution:** Examine domain names and subdomains for character substitutions or visually similar characters that may be used to deceive users. Look out for instances where attackers replace "m" with "rn," or use homograph characters to mimic legitimate domains.

o **Verify Domain Ownership:** Use domain lookup tools to verify the ownership and registration details of the domain. Legitimate websites typically provide clear ownership information, while deceptive ones may hide or obfuscate this data.

2. Browser Developer Tools:

   o **Inspect Page Elements:** In addition to examining the page source code, inspect other page elements using developer tools. Pay attention to the structure and layout of the page. Deceptive websites may have irregularities in the arrangement of elements or inconsistent styling.

   o **Evaluate JavaScript Files:** Analyze the JavaScript files associated with the webpage. Check for obfuscated or minified code, as well as any scripts that interact with user input fields or perform data transmissions.

   o **Detect Hidden Elements:** Look for hidden form fields, iframes, or embedded scripts that may not be visible to the user but could facilitate data collection or other malicious activities.

3. Network Request Monitoring:

   o **Examine Data Transfers:** When monitoring network requests, focus on data transfers between the user's browser and external servers. Suspicious destinations may involve obscure domains, IPs from high-risk regions, or non-standard ports.

   o **Use Browser Extensions:** Consider using browser extensions or add-ons specifically designed to enhance web security. Some extensions can automatically flag or block connections to known deceptive websites based on a continuously updated database of threats.

4. Security Headers:

   o **HTTP Strict Transport Security (HSTS):** Verify if the website uses HSTS headers, which ensure that the connection to the site is secure and encrypted. The absence of HSTS on a website that handles sensitive data may raise concerns.

   o **Content Security Policy (CSP):** Check for the presence of CSP headers, which define which scripts and resources are allowed to execute on the page. Properly configured CSP headers help protect against malicious script injections.

5.   Utilize Security Solutions Like Panoplia.io and others
     o   There are a few authentic cybersecurity ones using Artificial Intelligence and Machine Learning like Panoplia.io, Avast and others. They differ in their offerings and it is best to go to their website and evaluate what works best for you.
     o   By employing these advanced technical analysis techniques and leveraging security solutions like Panoply.io, users can significantly enhance their ability to spot and defend against deceptive websites. Staying vigilant and continuously updating one's cybersecurity knowledge is essential in the ever-evolving landscape of online threats.

The Dark Web: Unmasking Illicit Activities

The internet is a vast realm that offers access to information, communication, and commerce. However, beneath the surface lies a hidden layer known as the Dark Web, notorious for hosting a range of illicit activities. This chapter sheds light on this enigmatic part of the internet and explores the depths of its underground world.

Unveiling the Dark Web

The Dark Web is a segment of the internet that is intentionally hidden and inaccessible through traditional search engines. It requires specialized software like Tor (The Onion Router) to access its hidden services. While the Dark Web is not inherently illegal, it has gained infamy for being a haven for various unlawful activities.

Illicit Activities on the Dark Web

- **Illegal Marketplaces:** Dark Web marketplaces offer a plethora of illegal goods, from drugs and firearms to stolen data and counterfeit currencies. These marketplaces operate with a degree of anonymity, making it challenging for law enforcement to trace transactions.
- **Cybercrime Services:** Cybercriminals frequent the Dark Web to purchase or rent hacking tools, stolen credentials, and hacking services. This enables them to carry out cyberattacks on unsuspecting individuals and organizations.

- **Hacking Forums:** The Dark Web hosts forums where cybercriminals discuss hacking techniques, share vulnerabilities, and collaborate on malicious activities. These forums provide a breeding ground for cybercrime innovation.
- **Child Exploitation:** Disturbingly, the Dark Web is also known for hosting child exploitation content. Criminals use encrypted channels to share and distribute illegal materials, evading law enforcement efforts.

Cryptocurrency and Anonymity

Cryptocurrencies, like Bitcoin, are the preferred form of payment on the Dark Web due to their pseudonymous nature. Transactions made in cryptocurrencies provide a level of anonymity that traditional financial systems lack. This makes it difficult to trace the flow of funds and the identities of individuals involved in illicit transactions.

Legal and Ethical Dilemmas

The Dark Web raises complex legal and ethical questions. While it offers a degree of anonymity that can be vital for privacy, it is also a breeding ground for criminal activities. Law enforcement faces challenges in tackling crimes on the Dark Web due to the encrypted and decentralized nature of its operations.

Law Enforcement Efforts

Governments and law enforcement agencies around the world have intensified efforts to monitor and combat illicit activities on the Dark Web. Operation Onymous and AlphaBay takedown are examples of successful operations that disrupted major Dark Web marketplaces. However, the battle against the Dark Web's criminal underbelly is ongoing.

Navigating the Dark Web

Exploring the Dark Web is not advisable for the average user. Beyond the veil of anonymity lies a treacherous landscape of illegal activities and potential threats. Individuals should prioritize their digital safety and avoid engaging with the Dark Web.

The Dark Web remains a mysterious and controversial aspect of the internet. It serves as a reminder of the duality of technology – a tool that can empower individuals while also providing a refuge for criminal elements. As technology continues to evolve, society must grapple with the challenges posed by the Dark Web and collectively work towards a safer digital landscape.

Cryptocurrency and Its Role in Cybercrime

The emergence of cryptocurrency, particularly Bitcoin, has revolutionized the financial landscape by introducing a decentralized digital form of money. While cryptocurrencies hold promise for various legitimate applications, they have also become a pivotal tool for cybercriminals. This chapter delves into the intricate relationship between cryptocurrency and cybercrime, exploring how these digital currencies are exploited for nefarious activities.

The Appeal of Cryptocurrency for Cybercriminals

Cryptocurrencies offer a level of anonymity and pseudonymity that traditional financial systems lack. Transactions are conducted on decentralized ledgers, making it difficult to trace the identities of individuals involved. This characteristic has attracted cybercriminals, as it provides them with a means to conduct illicit transactions without the risk of easy detection.

Ransomware and Extortion

One of the most prominent uses of cryptocurrency in cybercrime is ransomware attacks. Malicious actors encrypt victims' data and demand a ransom payment, often in Bitcoin, to provide the decryption key. Cryptocurrencies enable these transactions to occur without revealing the identities of both parties, making it challenging for law enforcement to track the culprits.

Dark Web Marketplaces

The Dark Web is fueled by cryptocurrencies. It hosts numerous marketplaces where illegal goods and services are bought and sold using cryptocurrencies. From drugs and firearms to stolen data and hacking services, these marketplaces thrive due to the privacy and anonymity that cryptocurrencies provide.

Money Laundering and Fraud

Cryptocurrencies are exploited for money laundering and fraud schemes. Cybercriminals use mixers and tumblers to obfuscate the origin of funds, making it difficult to trace the flow of money. Ponzi schemes and investment frauds that promise high returns are also facilitated by cryptocurrencies, attracting unsuspecting investors.

ICO Scams and Pump-and-Dump Schemes

Initial Coin Offerings (ICOs) provide a legitimate way for projects to raise funds through the issuance of new cryptocurrencies. However, the lack of regulation has given rise to fraudulent ICOs that promise innovative projects but disappear after raising funds. Similarly, pump-and-dump schemes manipulate the value of a cryptocurrency by artificially inflating its price, only to leave investors with losses.

Darknet Marketplaces and Silk Road

Silk Road, the infamous darknet marketplace, is a testament to the interchapter of cryptocurrencies and cybercrime. Operating from 2011 to 2013, Silk Road facilitated illegal transactions worth billions of dollars, including drug sales and illegal services. Bitcoin was the preferred currency on Silk Road due to its anonymity, enabling users to conduct transactions beyond the reach of authorities.

Combatting Cryptocurrency-Enabled Cybercrime

The anonymity provided by cryptocurrencies poses challenges for law enforcement agencies. However, efforts are being made to track and combat cryptocurrency-related cybercrime. Blockchain analytics firms are working to trace transactions and identify patterns associated with illicit activities. Cryptocurrency exchanges are also subject to regulations to prevent money laundering and fraud.

Balancing Innovation and Regulation

As the use of cryptocurrencies in cybercrime grows, governments and regulatory bodies are grappling with striking a balance between innovation and oversight. While cryptocurrencies hold immense potential for innovation and financial inclusion, their misuse for illicit activities demands regulatory measures to curb cybercrime.

Cryptocurrency's role in cybercrime underscores the complexity of technology's impact on society. While digital currencies offer unprecedented benefits, they also provide new avenues for criminal exploitation. Effective solutions must encompass a combination of technology, regulation, and awareness to ensure the positive potential of cryptocurrencies prevails over their negative implications in the realm of cybercrime.

Chapter 4

PROTECTING YOURSELF ONLINE

Basic Cyber Hygiene and Best Practices

In today's interconnected world, practicing good cyber hygiene is paramount to safeguarding our digital lives. Cybercriminals are relentless in their pursuit of exploiting vulnerabilities, making it essential for individuals to be proactive in protecting themselves online. This chapter delves into the core principles of basic cyber hygiene and best practices that can help mitigate the risks of falling victim to cyber threats.

Understanding Cyber Hygiene

Cyber hygiene refers to the set of practices aimed at maintaining the health and security of our digital presence. Just as personal hygiene prevents physical ailments, cyber hygiene prevents digital infections that can compromise our sensitive information, financial stability, and overall online well-being.

Strong and Unique Passwords

Passwords are the first line of defense against unauthorized access. Create strong, unique passwords for each account, combining upper and lower case letters, numbers, and special characters. Avoid using easily guessable information like birthdays or names.

Multi-Factor Authentication (MFA)

MFA adds an extra layer of security by requiring multiple forms of verification, such as a password and a one-time code sent to your phone. Even if a cybercriminal obtains your password, MFA prevents them from accessing your accounts.

Regular Software Updates

Software updates are not just about new features; they often include critical security patches. Keep your operating system, applications, and antivirus software up to date to prevent exploitation of known vulnerabilities.

Beware of Phishing Attacks

Phishing attacks trick users into divulging sensitive information or clicking on malicious links. Be cautious of unsolicited emails, especially those asking for personal or financial information. Verify the legitimacy of the sender before taking any action.

Secure Wi-Fi Connections

Public Wi-Fi networks are often insecure and susceptible to eavesdropping. Avoid accessing sensitive information or making online transactions on public networks. Use a virtual private network (VPN) to encrypt your internet connection.

Privacy Settings

Review the privacy settings of your social media accounts and online profiles. Limit the amount of personal information you share publicly to minimize the risk of identity theft and social engineering attacks.

Secure Online Transactions

When making online transactions or purchases, ensure that the website uses secure connections (look for "https://" in the URL) and has a valid SSL certificate. Avoid sharing sensitive information over unsecured networks.

Regular Backups

Regularly back up your data to an external storage device or cloud service. In case of ransomware attacks or hardware failures, backups ensure that you can restore your files without paying a ransom.

Use Caution with Links and Attachments

Avoid clicking on links or opening attachments in unsolicited emails or messages. Cybercriminals often use these tactics to spread malware or trick users into revealing sensitive information.

Educate Yourself

Stay informed about the latest cyber threats and scams. Knowledge is your best defense against evolving cybercriminal tactics.

Adopting these fundamental cyber hygiene practices significantly reduces the risk of falling victim to cyber threats. Online safety is a shared responsibility, and by implementing these best practices, individuals can create a more secure digital environment for themselves and contribute to a safer online ecosystem overall. Remember, cyber hygiene is not a one-time effort but an ongoing commitment to protecting your digital life.

Strong Password Management, Two-Factor Authentication, and Biometrics: A Comprehensive Approach to Digital Security

In the dynamic landscape of cybersecurity, the battle between digital defenders and cybercriminals rages on. One of the foundational pillars of defense is robust authentication and access control. This chapter delves into the importance of strong password management, the significance of two-factor authentication (2FA), and the evolution of biometrics as advanced security measures.

The Power of Strong Passwords

Passwords are the keys to our digital lives. They grant access to our sensitive information, financial accounts, and personal data. Yet, many individuals still underestimate the importance of creating and maintaining strong passwords.

A strong password is characterized by its complexity and uniqueness. It combines upper- and lower-case letters, numbers, and special characters to create a virtually unbreakable barrier against brute-force attacks. It should be unrelated to easily discoverable personal information, such as birthdays or names.

Challenges of Password Management

The challenge with strong passwords lies in their complexity. Memorizing multiple complex passwords for different accounts can be daunting. This is where the importance of password management tools comes into play. Password managers are digital vaults that securely store your passwords and automatically fill them in when needed.

Password managers offer several advantages:

1. **Complexity:** They generate and store intricate passwords for each account.
2. **Convenience:** Users need to remember only the master password for the password manager.
3. **Security:** Data is encrypted, and many password managers offer features like biometric login.

Two-Factor Authentication (2FA)

While strong passwords are a significant step, they alone may not suffice. This is where two-factor authentication (2FA) or multi-factor authentication (MFA) steps in. 2FA adds an extra layer of security by requiring users to provide two or more forms of identification before accessing an account.

Typically, 2FA combines something you know (password) with something you have (e.g., a code sent to your phone) or something you are (biometric data). This dual verification process significantly reduces the risk of unauthorized access.

Biometrics: The Future of Authentication

As technology advances, the fusion of biology and technology emerges as a potent authentication method. Biometric authentication uses unique physical or behavioral characteristics, such as fingerprints, facial recognition, or even voice patterns, to grant access.

Biometric authentication offers several benefits:

1. **Inherent uniqueness:** Biometric traits are unique to individuals, making them difficult to replicate.
2. **Convenience:** No need to remember passwords or carry physical tokens.
3. **Enhanced security:** Biometric data is difficult to forge, making it a robust security measure.

Challenges and Considerations

Despite the advantages, biometric authentication also presents challenges. Biometric data can be compromised, and there are concerns about privacy and the potential for misuse. Additionally, biometric systems require advanced hardware, which may not be universally accessible.

Combining Forces for Ultimate Security

The convergence of strong password management, 2FA, and biometrics creates a multi-layered defense against cyber threats. When implemented together, these methods create a formidable barrier that discourages even the most determined cybercriminals.

In the realm of cybersecurity, passwords are the front gate to your digital kingdom. Ensuring their strength and fortifying them with additional layers of security like 2FA and biometrics creates a defense that is challenging for cybercriminals to breach. As we navigate the digital landscape, the importance of maintaining these layers of security cannot be overstated. Strong password management, coupled with 2FA and biometrics, empowers users to take control of their digital identities and safeguard their online lives.

Securing Personal Devices and Data: A Fundamental Approach to Digital Safety

In the digital age, our personal devices have become extensions of ourselves. From smartphones to laptops, these tools grant us access to a world of information and connectivity. However, this convenience comes with a significant responsibility: protecting our personal devices and the sensitive data they hold from the ever-present threat of cybercrime.

Understanding the Risks

Our personal devices store a wealth of sensitive information: from personal photos and emails to financial data and login credentials. Cybercriminals constantly seek to exploit vulnerabilities in these devices to gain unauthorized access and potentially wreak havoc in our lives.

Best Practices for Device Security

- **Regular Updates:** Keep your device's operating system and applications up to date. Updates often include security patches that address vulnerabilities.

- **Strong Passwords and Biometrics:** Set strong and unique passwords for each device and use biometric authentication methods where available.
- **Device Encryption:** Enable device encryption to ensure that even if your device is lost or stolen, your data remains inaccessible without the decryption key.
- **App Permissions:** Be cautious about granting permissions to apps. Only provide necessary access and review permissions regularly.
- **Download from Trusted Sources:** Only download apps and software from official app stores or reputable websites.
- **Avoid Public Wi-Fi:** Be cautious when using public Wi-Fi networks. If you must use them, consider using a virtual private network (VPN) to encrypt your connection.
- **Backup Your Data:** Regularly back up your device's data to a secure location. This ensures that even in case of a security breach, your data remains safe.

Protecting Personal Data

- **Strong Authentication:** Use strong, unique passwords for each online account and enable two-factor authentication (2FA) whenever possible.
- **Privacy Settings:** Review the privacy settings of your accounts and devices to control the information you share.
- **Avoid Phishing:** Be cautious of unsolicited emails, messages, or calls asking for personal information. Verify the source before responding.
- **Secure Browsing:** Use secure connections (https) and consider using a browser extension that blocks malicious websites.
- **Data Sharing:** Be mindful of what you share on social media. Cybercriminals can use personal information to craft targeted attacks.

Mobile Devices: Unique Considerations

Mobile devices pose specific challenges due to their portability and the vast amount of personal information they store. To enhance mobile device security:

- **Lock Screen Security:** Set a strong PIN, password, or biometric authentication for your device's lock screen.

- **Remote Wipe:** Enable remote wipe capabilities to erase your device's data in case it's lost or stolen.
- **App Permissions:** Regularly review and manage app permissions to prevent unnecessary access.
- **App Downloads:** Download apps only from official app stores, and read reviews before installing.
- **Securing Emails:** Use encrypted email services to protect sensitive email communication.

Securing personal devices and data is not a one-time task; it's an ongoing commitment to digital hygiene. By following best practices and staying informed about emerging threats, individuals can significantly reduce their vulnerability to cyberattacks. Remember, the protection of your personal devices and data ultimately rests in your hands. Safeguarding them not only shields you from cyber threats but also contributes to a safer and more secure digital ecosystem for everyone.

Safe Browsing Habits and Identifying Scams: Navigating the Digital Landscape

In today's digital world, safe browsing habits are essential for protecting yourself from a vast array of online threats. From phishing scams to malicious websites, cybercriminals are adept at using the internet to exploit unsuspecting users. Adopting safe browsing practices and learning to identify potential scams is crucial for staying secure online.

Safe Browsing Practices

- **HTTPS and Secure Sites:** Always look for "https://" at the beginning of a website's URL. This indicates that the connection is encrypted, making it harder for attackers to intercept your data.
- **Beware of Pop-ups:** Avoid clicking on pop-up ads or links that appear suspicious. Legitimate websites rarely use pop-ups to gather information.
- **Be Cautious with Email Links:** Do not click on links in emails from unknown senders. Even if an email appears to be from a familiar source, verify the URL before clicking.

- **Hover Before Clicking:** Hover your mouse pointer over a link to preview the URL before clicking. This helps you verify the link's authenticity.
- **Update Your Browser:** Keep your web browser updated to ensure that you have the latest security features and patches.
- **Use Ad Blockers:** Install ad blockers to reduce the risk of malicious ads leading to fraudulent websites.

Identifying Scams

- **Too Good to Be True:** Be skeptical of offers that seem too good to be true, such as winning a lottery you didn't enter or receiving unexpected gifts.
- **Urgent Requests:** Scammers often create a sense of urgency, urging you to take immediate action. Be cautious of requests for urgent payments or providing sensitive information.
- **Check the Source:** Verify the sender's email address before clicking on links or downloading attachments. Spoofed email addresses are a common tactic used by cybercriminals.
- **Spelling and Grammar:** Poor spelling and grammar in emails or on websites can be a red flag for scams.
- **Unsolicited Requests:** Be wary of unsolicited communications asking for personal or financial information.

Common Online Scams

- **Phishing Emails:** Scammers send emails impersonating legitimate institutions to trick users into revealing personal information or login credentials.
- **Tech Support Scams:** Cybercriminals pose as tech support agents, claiming your device has a virus. They then offer to "fix" the issue for a fee.
- **Online Shopping Scams:** Fake online stores offer products at unbelievable prices. Once payments are made, the products never arrive.
- **Social Engineering:** Scammers manipulate users into providing sensitive information by exploiting emotions, such as sympathy or fear.
- **Investment Scams:** Fraudulent investment opportunities promise high returns but end up being Ponzi schemes.

Staying Informed

- **Educate Yourself:** Stay informed about the latest online threats and scams. Knowledge is your best defense against cybercriminals.
- **Trust Your Instincts:** If something doesn't feel right, trust your instincts and verify before taking any action.
- **Keep Software Updated:** Regularly update your operating system, browser, and security software to stay protected against known vulnerabilities.

Safe browsing habits and the ability to identify scams are critical skills in the digital age. By adopting a cautious approach, verifying the authenticity of websites and emails, and staying informed about common online scams, you can significantly reduce your risk of falling victim to cybercriminals. Remember, your online safety is in your hands, and a little vigilance can go a long way in ensuring a secure digital experience.

Recognizing Suspicious Emails and Links: Unmasking Digital Deceit

Email has become an integral part of our daily lives, offering convenience and instant communication. However, it has also become a breeding ground for cybercriminals who utilize it to execute a variety of online scams. Recognizing suspicious emails and links is a vital skill to safeguard yourself and your digital identity from these threats.

Anatomy of a Phishing Email

- **Sender's Address:** Scammers often use email addresses that resemble legitimate ones with slight alterations. Always check the sender's email address carefully.
- **Urgent Tone:** Phishing emails create a sense of urgency, pressuring recipients to act quickly without thinking.
- **Generic Greetings:** Scammers use generic salutations like "Dear Customer" instead of using your name.
- **Suspicious URLs:** Hover over links without clicking to see the actual URL. Be wary of misspellings or slight variations of legitimate domains.

- **Spelling and Grammar:** Poor language skills in an email could indicate a phishing attempt.

Recognizing Suspicious Links

- **Unsolicited Links:** Be cautious of links received from unknown sources, especially in emails or messages.
- **URL Shorteners:** Cybercriminals often use URL shorteners to hide the true destination of a link. Use online tools to expand and preview shortened URLs.
- **Mismatched URLs:** Verify that the link's displayed text matches its actual URL. Scammers may use hyperlinked text that doesn't lead to the expected webpage.
- **HTTPS Encryption:** Always check for the "https://" prefix in URLs, indicating a secure connection.

Examples of Phishing Scams

- **Fake Account Alerts:** Scammers send emails pretending to be from banks or service providers, claiming there's a problem with your account and urging you to click a link to resolve it.
- **Fake Invoices or Orders:** Phishing emails may appear as invoices or order confirmations, tricking recipients into clicking malicious links or downloading malware.
- **Emergency Requests:** Emails claiming to be from a friend or relative in trouble ask for money urgently, playing on emotions to elicit a response.
- **IRS Scams:** Emails that impersonate tax authorities threaten legal action unless immediate payment is made, prompting victims to disclose financial information.

Preventive Measures

- **Verify Sender:** Always confirm the legitimacy of the sender before responding to any email requests or clicking links.
- **Avoid Clicking:** If an email contains links or attachments you weren't expecting, avoid clicking them.

- **Double-Check URLs:** Manually type URLs instead of clicking links to ensure you're visiting the correct website.
- **Use Security Software:** Install reputable antivirus and anti-malware software to detect and block phishing attempts.
- **Educate Yourself:** Stay informed about the latest phishing techniques and scams to enhance your ability to recognize them.

In the ever-evolving landscape of cyber threats, recognizing suspicious emails and links is paramount. By cultivating a skeptical mindset, verifying sender identities, scrutinizing URLs, and educating yourself about common phishing tactics, you can shield yourself from the deceitful tactics of cybercriminals. Remember, a cautious approach in the digital realm can save you from the potential havoc caused by falling victim to phishing scams.

Chapter 5

RESPONDING TO CYBER ATTACKS

Steps to Take After Falling for a Scam

In the fast-paced digital world, cyber attacks have become an unfortunate reality. Despite our best efforts to stay vigilant, even the most cautious individuals may find themselves falling victim to a cyber scam. While the initial realization of being duped can be distressing, it's crucial to act swiftly and strategically to mitigate further damage. In this chapter, we will discuss the essential steps to take after falling for a scam, empowering you with the knowledge to respond effectively.

Step 1: Stay Calm and Gather Information

The first and most critical step is to remain calm. Panic can cloud judgment and hinder your ability to respond effectively. Take a moment to gather all relevant information about the scam, including emails, messages, or any other communication involved. This information will be crucial when reporting the incident to relevant authorities.

Step 2: Secure Your Accounts

Change the passwords of all compromised accounts immediately. Use strong, unique passwords that are not easily guessable. If you have fallen for a phishing attack, notify your bank, credit card company, or any financial institution that may be affected. Be sure to monitor your accounts closely for any unauthorized transactions.

Step 3: Report the Scam

Report the scam to the appropriate authorities. This could include local law enforcement, the cybercrime department, or relevant consumer protection agencies. If the scam involved a fake website or social media account, report it to the platform's administrators.

Step 4: Inform Your Contacts
If the scam involved sending malicious links or content to your contacts, inform them immediately. Cybercriminals often use compromised accounts to spread malware or further phishing attacks.

Step 5: Monitor Your Personal Information
Keep a close eye on your personal information, such as your credit report, bank statements, and online accounts. Cybercriminals may attempt identity theft or unauthorized transactions using the information they have obtained.

Step 6: Install Security Software
Make sure your devices are equipped with up-to-date security software. This will help identify and prevent future cyber threats.

Step 7: Learn from the Experience
While falling for a scam is unfortunate, it can also be a valuable learning experience. Understand the tactics that scammers used and educate yourself to recognize similar schemes in the future.

Step 8: Educate Others
Share your experience with friends and family to raise awareness about common cyber scams. By sharing your story, you may prevent others from falling victim to the same tactics.

Responding to a cyber-attack with a clear mind and a systematic approach can significantly minimize the impact of the incident. By taking these steps, you can regain control of the situation, protect your personal information, and contribute to a safer online environment for yourself and others. Remember, even the most cautious individuals can be targeted, but with the right response, you can effectively navigate the aftermath of a cyber scam.

Reporting Cybercrimes and Scammers: Legal Aspects of Cyber Frauds

As the digital landscape continues to evolve, so do the tactics and techniques employed by cybercriminals. The rise of cybercrimes and scams has prompted governments, law enforcement agencies, and legal experts to adapt and respond to these new challenges. In this chapter, we will delve into the critical topic of reporting cybercrimes and scammers, as well as explore the legal aspects surrounding cyber frauds.

Reporting Cybercrimes: A Collaborative Effort

Reporting cybercrimes and scams is a collective effort that involves individuals, businesses, law enforcement agencies, and governmental bodies. The ability to report such incidents is essential for several reasons:

1. **Victim Assistance:** Reporting cybercrimes allows victims to receive appropriate guidance and assistance. Law enforcement agencies can provide advice on how to mitigate damage, secure compromised accounts, and prevent future incidents.
2. **Data Collection:** Reporting incidents provides valuable data to law enforcement and cybersecurity agencies. Analyzing this data helps identify trends, tactics, and the scale of cybercrimes, enabling more effective prevention and response strategies.
3. **Legal Action:** Reporting cybercrimes can lead to legal action against perpetrators. Timely reporting ensures that law enforcement can gather evidence and build a case against the criminals.

How to Report Cybercrimes:

1. **Local Law Enforcement:** For immediate threats or if you have suffered financial losses due to cybercrimes, contact your local law enforcement agency.
2. **Cybercrime Units:** Many countries have specialized cybercrime units within their law enforcement agencies. These units are equipped to handle complex cyber investigations.
3. **National Cybersecurity Agencies:** In some cases, national cybersecurity agencies are responsible for investigating and combating cybercrimes. They can provide guidance on reporting incidents.

4. **Online Reporting Platforms:** Some countries offer online platforms for reporting cybercrimes. These platforms make it easier to provide detailed information about the incident.

Legal Aspects of Cyber Frauds

Cybercrimes often span across geographical boundaries, making legal jurisdiction and prosecution complex. However, several legal aspects are crucial in addressing cyber frauds:

1. **Legislation:** Many countries have enacted specific legislation to address cybercrimes. These laws define cybercrimes, their penalties, and legal procedures for investigation and prosecution.
2. **Extradition:** Given the global nature of cybercrimes, extradition treaties are essential for bringing criminals to justice across borders.
3. **International Cooperation:** Law enforcement agencies collaborate internationally to combat cybercrimes. International organizations facilitate sharing of information, expertise, and resources.
4. **Digital Evidence:** Collecting and preserving digital evidence is crucial for prosecution. Courts increasingly rely on digital evidence to establish guilt or innocence.
5. **Privacy Concerns:** Balancing the need to investigate cybercrimes with individuals' right to privacy is a challenge. Laws often specify the circumstances under which authorities can access personal data.

Conclusion: A Unified Front Against Cybercrimes:

As technology advances, so do the methods of cybercriminals. Reporting cybercrimes and understanding the legal aspects surrounding them are pivotal in tackling this evolving threat. Governments, law enforcement agencies, and individuals must work together to build a secure digital ecosystem. By promptly reporting incidents and adhering to legal procedures, we contribute to safeguarding our digital lives and fostering a safer online environment for all.

Cybersecurity for Small Businesses: Safeguarding the Digital Realm

- **Resource Constraints:** Small businesses often have limited financial resources allocated to cybersecurity. They may prioritize other operational expenses over investing in robust security measures. As a result, they may not have the latest security tools, technologies, or dedicated cybersecurity personnel, making them more susceptible to attacks.

- **Lack of Awareness:** Many small business owners may not fully understand the extent of cyber threats or the potential impact on their operations. This lack of awareness can lead to complacency regarding cybersecurity practices. Small business owners may not see the value in cybersecurity training or may underestimate the prevalence of cyberattacks targeted at businesses of their size.

- **Vendors and Third Parties:** Small businesses often rely on vendors, suppliers, and third-party service providers. These external entities may handle sensitive data or interact with the business's systems, creating potential vulnerabilities. Small businesses may not have the leverage or resources to enforce stringent cybersecurity standards on these partners, leaving them exposed to risks stemming from third-party breaches.

- **Rapid Growth:** Small businesses that experience rapid growth may struggle to adapt their cybersecurity posture accordingly. As they expand, they add more digital assets, devices, and users to their network. Without adequate cybersecurity planning and resources, this rapid scaling can lead to security gaps and vulnerabilities that cybercriminals can exploit.

- **Compliance and Regulations:** Depending on the industry and location, small businesses may be subject to various data protection and cybersecurity regulations. Navigating these compliance requirements can be challenging, especially if they lack dedicated compliance officers or legal counsel. Non-compliance can result in legal and financial repercussions.

- **Employee Training:** Small businesses may not prioritize cybersecurity training for their employees. Without proper training, employees may inadvertently engage in risky online behavior, such as clicking on phishing emails or using weak passwords, which can expose the business to cyber threats.

Strategies to Protect Small Businesses:

Given these challenges, small businesses can implement several strategies to safeguard their digital assets:

1. **Security Awareness Training:** Invest in cybersecurity education and training for employees to raise awareness about cyber threats and best practices. Regular training sessions can empower employees to recognize and report potential risks.

2. **Managed Security Services:** Consider outsourcing cybersecurity to managed security service providers (MSSPs) that offer cost-effective security solutions. MSSPs can provide 24/7 monitoring, threat detection, and incident response, alleviating the burden on internal resources.

3. **Patch Management:** Keep software, operating systems, and applications up to date with the latest security patches. Cybercriminals often target known vulnerabilities, so timely patching is critical.

4. **Strong Password Policies:** Enforce strong password policies and encourage the use of password managers. Implement two-factor authentication (2FA) wherever possible to add an extra layer of security.

5. **Regular Backups:** Implement a robust backup and disaster recovery plan to mitigate the impact of data breaches or ransomware attacks. Regularly test backups to ensure data integrity.

6. **Vendor Assessment:** Evaluate the cybersecurity practices of vendors and third-party partners. Ensure they adhere to security standards and are capable of protecting shared data.

7. **Incident Response Plan:** Develop a well-defined incident response plan that outlines steps to take in case of a cyber incident. This plan should include communication protocols, containment measures, and recovery procedures.

8. **Cyber Insurance:** Consider purchasing cyber insurance to help mitigate the financial impact of a cyberattack or data breach. Cyber insurance policies can cover various expenses, including legal fees and customer notification costs.

9. **Compliance Adherence:** Stay informed about relevant data protection and privacy regulations. Ensure compliance with applicable laws to avoid legal penalties.

10. **Regular Security Audits:** Conduct periodic security audits or assessments to identify vulnerabilities and areas for improvement in your cybersecurity posture.

Small businesses play a vital role in the global economy, and their cybersecurity is crucial to safeguarding their operations, reputation, and customer trust. By addressing the unique challenges they face and implementing proactive security measures, small businesses can significantly reduce their vulnerability to cyber threats.

Chapter 6

CYBERSECURITY FOR DIFFERENT PERSONAS

Cybersecurity is not a one-size-fits-all endeavor. It requires tailored approaches to address the unique needs, challenges, and risks faced by different personas in our increasingly digital world. In this chapter, we will delve into the cybersecurity considerations and best practices for various personas, ranging from digital enthusiasts to healthcare professionals. Each group encounters distinct digital environments, threats, and opportunities, necessitating targeted strategies to safeguard their online presence and data.

Digital Enthusiasts

Digital enthusiasts, often early adopters of technology, possess an inherent passion for all things digital. Their active engagement with the digital world exposes them to both the latest trends and the newest cybersecurity threats. To ensure a secure online experience for digital enthusiasts, the following cybersecurity practices should be adopted:

1. Continuous Learning:
   - **Stay Informed:** Cyber threats evolve rapidly, so digital enthusiasts should stay informed about the latest cybersecurity threats, vulnerabilities, and attack techniques. Following cybersecurity news websites, blogs, and social media accounts of cybersecurity experts can provide valuable insights.
   - **Online Courses and Certifications:** Consider enrolling in cybersecurity courses or obtaining certifications like Certified Information Systems Security Professional (CISSP) or Certified Ethical Hacker (CEH) to gain a deeper understanding of cybersecurity principles.

2. Multi-Factor Authentication (MFA):
   - **Enable MFA on all Online Accounts:** MFA adds an extra layer of security by requiring users to provide two or more verification factors before granting access to an account. This significantly enhances security and helps protect against unauthorized access.

3. Privacy Settings:
   - **Regularly Review and Adjust Privacy Settings:** Social media platforms and online services often update their privacy settings. Digital enthusiasts should routinely review and adjust these settings to control who can see their information and limit exposure to potential threats.

4. Secure Devices:
   - **Keep Devices and Software Updated:** Regularly update operating systems, applications, and software to patch known vulnerabilities. Cybercriminals often target unpatched systems.
   - **Use Reputable App Stores:** Download apps and software only from official app stores, such as Google Play Store or Apple App Store, to minimize the risk of downloading malicious apps.
   - **Install Antivirus and Anti-Malware Software:** Use reputable antivirus and anti-malware solutions to protect devices from known threats.

5. Encryption:
   - **Employ Encryption Tools:** For sensitive communications, use end-to-end encryption tools like Signal, WhatsApp, or Telegram to ensure that messages and data are secure during transit.
   - **Secure Wi-Fi Networks:** Use strong and unique passwords for Wi-Fi networks, and consider using a virtual private network (VPN) when connecting to public Wi-Fi networks to encrypt internet traffic.

6. Backup Data:
   - **Regularly Back Up Data:** Implement automated backups of important files and data to an external device or cloud storage. In case of a cyberattack or data loss, having up-to-date backups can be a lifesaver.

7. Secure Password Management:
   - **Use Strong, Unique Passwords:** Generate complex passwords for each online account and store them securely using a reputable password manager. Avoid using easily guessable information such as birthdays or common words.
   - **Enable Two-Factor Authentication (2FA):** Whenever possible, enable 2FA for online accounts to provide an extra layer of security.

8. Safe Online Shopping:
   - **Verify Online Retailers:** Before making online purchases, ensure that the retailer's website is legitimate and secure. Look for "https://" in the URL and a padlock icon in the address bar.
   - **Be Cautious with Personal Information:** Avoid sharing unnecessary personal information during online shopping, and use credit cards rather than debit cards for added fraud protection.

By adopting these cybersecurity practices, digital enthusiasts can continue to explore the digital realm with confidence, knowing they have taken proactive steps to protect their online presence and data from cyber threats. Staying informed, being vigilant, and maintaining good cyber hygiene are essential components of a secure digital lifestyle.

Older Generation

The older generation, while often less experienced with digital technology, is increasingly becoming a target for cybercriminals due to their potential vulnerabilities. To enhance the cybersecurity posture of older individuals, a multifaceted approach is needed that combines education, support, and vigilance:

1. Cyber Awareness Training:
    o   **Recognizing Online Scams:** Provide older individuals with education on recognizing common online scams and phishing attempts. This includes teaching them how to identify suspicious emails, messages, or websites that may be used to deceive them.
    o   **Phishing Awareness:** Emphasize the importance of never sharing personal or financial information via email or with unknown contacts. Make them aware of the tactics cybercriminals use to impersonate trusted entities.

2. Safe Browsing Practices:
    o   **Use Reputable Websites:** Encourage the use of well-established and reputable websites when shopping, banking, or seeking information. Older individuals should avoid clicking on links in unsolicited emails and instead navigate directly to websites by typing the URL in the browser.

- o **Avoid Suspicious Links:** Teach them to be cautious when encountering links in emails or messages, especially those claiming to be urgent or offering unbelievable deals. Advise them to hover over links to preview the destination URL before clicking.

3. Family Support:
   - o **Assist with Device Security:** Family members can assist older individuals in configuring security settings on their devices, such as enabling firewall and antivirus software. They should also ensure that operating systems and applications are regularly updated to patch vulnerabilities.
   - o **Provide Guidance:** Offer guidance on setting strong and unique passwords for online accounts. Encourage the use of password managers to simplify password management.
   - o **Secure Wi-Fi Networks:** Help them secure their home Wi-Fi networks with strong, unique passwords and encryption protocols. Explain the importance of using trusted and regularly updated routers.

4. Regular Check-Ins:
   - o **Address Concerns:** Establish a routine for regular check-ins or visits to address any cybersecurity concerns or issues. Older individuals may have questions or encounter unfamiliar situations online, so providing ongoing support and guidance is essential.
   - o **Update Software:** During these check-ins, ensure that all software, including antivirus programs and the operating system, is up to date. This minimizes the risk of exploitation through known vulnerabilities.

5. Safe Social Media Practices:
   - o **Privacy Settings:** Teach them how to adjust privacy settings on social media platforms to control who can see their posts and personal information.
   - o **Recognize Friend Requests:** Caution them to be skeptical of friend requests from unknown individuals and to verify the identity of the requester if necessary.

6. Email Security:
    o   **Attachments and Links:** Advise against opening email attachments or clicking on links in emails from unknown senders. Emphasize the potential dangers of downloading files from unverified sources.

7. Encourage Reporting:
    o   **Open Communication:** Foster an open and non-judgmental line of communication so that older individuals feel comfortable reporting any suspicious online activity or potential security breaches.
    o   **Reporting Scams:** Teach them how and where to report online scams and fraud, such as to local law enforcement, government agencies, or consumer protection organizations.

Cybersecurity for the older generation should focus on empowering them with knowledge, providing hands-on support, and fostering open communication with family members or caregivers. By following these practices and staying vigilant, older individuals can enjoy the benefits of the digital world while minimizing their exposure to online threats.

Parents with Young Kids

Parents with young children have the critical responsibility of safeguarding their kids in the digital realm. This entails not only ensuring the safety of their children online but also maintaining the security of their own digital environments. Cybersecurity for parents with young kids is multifaceted and includes the following key aspects:

1. Parental Control Software:
   o **Usage Monitoring:** Utilize parental control software to monitor your children's online activities. These tools allow you to track the websites they visit, the apps they use, and the amount of time spent online.
   o **Content Filtering:** Implement content filtering to restrict access to age-inappropriate or potentially harmful websites and applications. Parental control software typically enables parents to set up filtering rules based on age groups and content categories.

2. Educational and Age-Appropriate Content:
   o **Encourage Educational Engagement:** Promote the use of educational and age-appropriate content and apps. Look for digital resources that align with your child's educational needs and interests.
   o **App Selection:** Curate a selection of apps and games that not only entertain but also educate. Investigate app ratings, reviews, and educational value before allowing your child to use them.

3. Privacy Discussions:
   o **Educate About Online Privacy:** Initiate age-appropriate discussions with your children about online privacy and responsible internet use. Teach them about the potential risks associated with sharing personal information online.
   o **Responsible Sharing:** Emphasize the importance of not sharing personal details, such as full names, addresses, phone numbers, or school names, with strangers online. Teach your children to seek your guidance when sharing any personal information.

4. Secure Devices:
   o **Device Security:** Ensure that the devices used by your children, such as smartphones, tablets, or computers, are secure and regularly updated. Enable security features like PIN locks or biometric authentication to prevent unauthorized access.

- o **Antivirus Software:** Install and maintain antivirus or security software on devices to protect against malware and other digital threats.
- o **App Permissions:** Review and manage app permissions to restrict access to sensitive data, such as location or camera usage, for applications that do not require such access.

5. Safe Online Practices:
   - o **Supervision:** Supervise your children's online activities, especially for younger kids. Be present and engaged when they are using the internet.
   - o **Establish Rules:** Set clear rules and guidelines for screen time, online activities, and the use of social media platforms. Create a balanced digital environment that includes offline activities and face-to-face interactions.
   - o **Model Behavior:** Children often learn by observing their parents. Model responsible online behavior, including respectful communication and privacy awareness.

6. Regular Conversations:
   - o **Open Dialogue:** Maintain open and ongoing conversations with your children about their online experiences. Encourage them to share any concerns or uncomfortable encounters they may have had online.
   - o **Cyberbullying Awareness:** Teach your children about cyberbullying and its harmful effects. Make sure they know how to respond if they encounter or witness such behavior.

7. Emergency Response Plan:
   - o **Reporting Procedures:** Establish clear procedures for reporting any suspicious or uncomfortable interactions online. Ensure your children know how to reach out for help if they feel threatened or harassed.
   - o **Emergency Contacts:** Provide your children with emergency contact information, including phone numbers for parents, trusted family members, and local authorities.

8. Digital Literacy and Critical Thinking:
   - **Teach Digital Literacy:** Equip your children with digital literacy skills, including how to fact-check information, identify fake news, and critically assess online content for credibility.
   - **Online Etiquette:** Teach them about good online etiquette, emphasizing the importance of kindness, respect, and empathy when interacting with others on the internet.

9. Stay Informed:
   - **Keep Up with Technology:** Stay informed about the latest technology trends, social media platforms, and popular apps that your children may be using. This knowledge helps you better understand their online world.

10. Support Network:
    - **Engage with Other Parents:** Connect with other parents to share experiences, knowledge, and best practices in managing children's online activities. Joining parenting groups or forums can provide valuable insights.

11. Periodic Reassessment:
    - **Review and Adjust:** Periodically review and adjust your cybersecurity measures and rules as your children grow and their digital needs change. Adapt to evolving technology and online trends.

12. Online Privacy Education:
    - **Privacy Protection:** Teach your children how to configure privacy settings on their devices and social media accounts. Encourage them to use strong, unique passwords and enable two-factor authentication where possible.

13. Emergency Response Plan:
    - **Reporting Procedures:** Establish clear procedures for reporting any suspicious or uncomfortable interactions online. Ensure your children know how to reach out for help if they feel threatened or harassed.
    - **Emergency Contacts:** Provide your children with emergency contact information, including phone numbers for parents, trusted family members, and local authorities.

14. Digital Literacy and Critical Thinking:
    - **Teach Digital Literacy:** Equip your children with digital literacy skills, including how to fact-check information, identify fake news, and critically assess online content for credibility.
    - **Online Etiquette:** Teach them about good online etiquette, emphasizing the importance of kindness, respect, and empathy when interacting with others on the internet.

15. Stay Informed:
    - **Keep Up with Technology:** Stay informed about the latest technology trends, social media platforms, and popular apps that your children may be using. This knowledge helps you better understand their online world.

16. Support Network:
    - **Engage with Other Parents:** Connect with other parents to share experiences, knowledge, and best practices in managing children's online activities. Joining parenting groups or forums can provide valuable insights.

17. Periodic Reassessment:
    - **Review and Adjust:** Periodically review and adjust your cybersecurity measures and rules as your children grow and their digital needs change. Adapt to evolving technology and online trends.

18. Online Privacy Education:
    - **Privacy Protection:** Teach your children how to configure privacy settings on their devices and social media accounts. Encourage them to use strong, unique passwords and enable two-factor authentication where possible.

By implementing these comprehensive cybersecurity practices, parents can create a safe and educational online environment for their young children while also protecting their family's digital well-being. It's essential to strike a balance between exploration and safety, allowing children to harness the positive aspects of the digital world while mitigating potential risks.

Rural Population

Cybersecurity considerations for rural populations come with a distinct set of challenges, primarily stemming from limited internet infrastructure and access to cybersecurity resources. These challenges make it crucial to implement tailored cybersecurity measures for rural communities. Here's an in-depth look at cybersecurity strategies for rural populations:

1. Internet Safety Workshops:
   o **Community Education:** Organize internet safety workshops and cybersecurity awareness programs tailored to the needs of rural residents. These workshops should cover topics such as recognizing online threats, safe online practices, and protecting personal information.
   o **Local Experts:** Invite local cybersecurity experts, law enforcement officials, or educators to conduct these workshops. Local presenters can relate cybersecurity concepts to the specific challenges faced by rural communities.

2. Access to Resources:
   o **Advocacy:** Advocate for improved internet infrastructure in rural areas. Collaborate with local government authorities, internet service providers (ISPs), and community organizations to address connectivity issues. Better internet access not only facilitates online activities but also enhances the ability to implement cybersecurity measures.
   o **Subsidized Security Tools:** Encourage government agencies and nonprofit organizations to provide subsidies or grants for cybersecurity tools and services. This can make essential cybersecurity resources more affordable and accessible to rural residents.

3. Local Support:
   o **Cybersecurity Networks:** Foster the development of local cybersecurity support networks or user groups within rural communities. These groups can serve as valuable resources for sharing information, discussing cybersecurity challenges, and providing assistance.

- **Partnerships:** Forge partnerships with nearby urban areas or organizations that specialize in cybersecurity. Collaborative efforts can extend cybersecurity expertise and resources to rural populations.

4. Community Engagement:
   - **Community Involvement:** Encourage active community involvement in cybersecurity initiatives. Rural residents should be encouraged to participate in local cybersecurity awareness campaigns, reporting of suspicious online activities, and sharing knowledge with neighbors.
   - **Neighborhood Watch Approach:** Promote a "neighborhood watch" approach to cybersecurity. Encourage residents to watch out for unusual online activities within their communities and report potential threats.

5. Local Cybersecurity Resources:
   - **Localized Resources:** Develop localized cybersecurity resources, such as guides, manuals, and contact lists for local cybersecurity experts. These resources should be easily accessible to rural residents.
   - **Local Helplines:** Establish local helplines or contact points for cybersecurity-related queries and assistance. Having a familiar and accessible point of contact can help rural residents address cybersecurity concerns effectively.

6. Government Support:
   - **Government Initiatives:** Collaborate with local and regional governments to create cybersecurity initiatives tailored to rural areas. These initiatives can include funding for cybersecurity programs, training for local law enforcement, and support for community-based cybersecurity projects.
   - **Regulatory Advocacy:** Advocate for policies that incentivize ISPs to invest in rural internet infrastructure and improve cybersecurity services in underserved areas.

7. Digital Literacy Programs:
   - **Basic Digital Skills:** Implement digital literacy programs that focus on teaching basic online skills to rural residents. Cover fundamental

concepts such as safe browsing, password management, and recognizing phishing attempts.

- o **Local Educational Institutions:** Partner with local schools and educational institutions to integrate cybersecurity awareness into the curriculum. Educating young rural residents about cybersecurity from an early age can have long-term benefits.

8. Community Watchdog Mentality:
    - o **Empower Residents:** Encourage a sense of responsibility for cybersecurity within rural communities. Promote the idea that residents play a vital role in safeguarding the digital well-being of the entire community.
    - o **Reporting Mechanisms:** Establish clear reporting mechanisms for cybersecurity incidents or concerns. Ensure that rural residents know how and where to report suspicious activities.

By focusing on these tailored cybersecurity strategies, rural communities can enhance their resilience to online threats and create a safer digital environment for their residents. These efforts not only protect individuals but also contribute to the overall cybersecurity posture of rural regions.

Educational Institutions

Educational institutions, including schools, colleges, and universities, are entrusted with sensitive student data and intellectual property. As cyber threats continue to evolve, these institutions face an increasing risk of cyberattacks. Implementing comprehensive cybersecurity measures is crucial to safeguard data, privacy, and the continuity of education. Here's an in-depth exploration of cybersecurity strategies for educational institutions:

1. Network Security:
    - o **Firewall Protection:** Deploy robust firewall solutions to monitor and filter incoming and outgoing network traffic. This helps block malicious connections and prevents unauthorized access to the network.
    - o **Intrusion Detection and Prevention Systems (IDPS):** Implement IDPS to detect and thwart suspicious network activities in real-time. These systems can identify potential threats and mitigate them swiftly.

- **Network Segmentation:** Divide the network into segments, restricting access to sensitive data and critical systems. This minimizes the lateral movement of attackers in case of a breach.
- **Regular Vulnerability Assessments:** Conduct frequent vulnerability assessments and penetration testing to identify weaknesses in the network infrastructure and address them promptly.

2. Data Encryption:
   - **Data-at-Rest Encryption:** Encrypt sensitive data stored on servers, databases, and portable devices. Data encryption ensures that even if attackers gain access to the data, it remains unreadable without the decryption keys.
   - **Secure Communication:** Implement encrypted communication channels for data transmission within the institution. Secure protocols like HTTPS should be used for websites, and secure email gateways should be deployed for email communications.

3. User Training:
   - **Cybersecurity Awareness Programs:** Develop and execute ongoing cybersecurity awareness programs for both staff and students. Training should cover topics such as recognizing phishing emails, creating strong passwords, and identifying social engineering tactics.
   - **Secure Password Practices:** Encourage the use of strong, unique passwords and the regular updating of passwords. Consider implementing password management tools for added security.

4. Incident Response:
   - **Incident Response Plan (IRP):** Establish a well-defined incident response plan that outlines the steps to take in case of a cyber incident or data breach. Ensure that staff members are trained in incident response procedures.
   - **Rapid Incident Detection:** Implement advanced threat detection solutions that can identify anomalies and suspicious activities on the network. Early detection is crucial for minimizing the impact of cyber incidents.

- o **Data Backup and Recovery:** Regularly back up all critical data and systems. Test data recovery processes to ensure business continuity in the event of data loss or system compromise.

5. Access Control and Authentication:
   - o **Role-Based Access Control (RBAC):** Implement RBAC to restrict user access based on their roles and responsibilities within the institution. Users should have the minimum necessary permissions to perform their tasks.
   - o **Multi-Factor Authentication (MFA):** Enforce MFA for accessing sensitive systems and applications. MFA adds an extra layer of security by requiring users to provide multiple forms of verification.

6. Software and Patch Management:
   - o **Regular Updates:** Keep all software, including operating systems and applications, up to date with security patches and updates. Vulnerabilities in outdated software can be exploited by cyber attackers.
   - o **Application Whitelisting:** Employ application whitelisting to allow only approved and trusted software to run on institutional systems. This prevents the execution of unauthorized or malicious programs.

7. Third-Party Vendors:
   - o **Vendor Assessment:** Assess the cybersecurity practices of third-party vendors, especially those providing educational software and cloud services. Ensure that they meet security standards and protect student data.

8. Data Privacy Compliance:
   - o **Compliance Measures:** Adhere to data privacy regulations and standards, such as the Family Educational Rights and Privacy Act (FERPA) in the United States. Ensure that sensitive student data is handled and stored in accordance with these regulations.

9. Security Awareness for Students:
   - o **Student Training:** Educate students about cybersecurity best practices and responsible online behavior. Teach them to recognize potential threats and report any security incidents to the institution.

10. Regular Security Audits:
    o **Independent Audits:** Conduct regular cybersecurity audits or hire independent cybersecurity firms to evaluate the institution's security posture objectively.

11. Collaboration and Information Sharing:
    o **Information Sharing Networks:** Join cybersecurity information sharing networks or consortia to stay informed about emerging threats and learn from the experiences of other educational institutions.

12. Secure Remote Learning:
    o **Remote Learning Security:** Extend cybersecurity measures to cover remote learning environments. Ensure that online learning platforms are secure and privacy-compliant.

13. Continual Improvement:
    o **Feedback Loops:** Establish feedback mechanisms for staff, students, and IT personnel to report security concerns or suggest improvements in cybersecurity measures.

By implementing these comprehensive cybersecurity strategies, educational institutions can create a secure digital environment for students, staff, and the institution's sensitive data. Protecting the integrity of educational institutions is not only essential for data privacy but also for maintaining the trust and reputation of the institution within the academic community.

Healthcare Professionals

Cybersecurity for healthcare professionals in India involves several specific considerations and compliance requirements in addition to the general best practices mentioned earlier:

1. Compliance with Indian Laws:
    o **Information Technology (Reasonable Security Practices and Procedures and Sensitive Personal Data or Information) Rules, 2011:** Healthcare professionals and organizations must adhere to these rules, which outline security practices and procedures for handling sensitive personal data or information (SPDI). Compliance includes the protection of SPDI and notification of data breaches.

2. Data Localization:
   o **Data Storage in India:** Consider data localization requirements, which mandate that certain types of data, especially sensitive health data, be stored within India's borders. Ensure that patient records are stored on servers located in India to comply with these regulations.

3. Aadhaar Compliance:
   o **Aadhaar Act:** If Aadhaar information (India's unique identification number) is part of healthcare records, ensure compliance with the Aadhaar Act, which regulates the use and protection of Aadhaar data.

4. State-Specific Regulations:
   o **State-Specific Laws:** Be aware of state-specific regulations related to healthcare data and privacy, as different Indian states may have their own rules and guidelines.

5. Telemedicine Regulations:
   o **Telemedicine Practice Guidelines:** If providing telemedicine services, follow the Telemedicine Practice Guidelines issued by the Indian Ministry of Health and Family Welfare. These guidelines cover the legal and ethical aspects of telemedicine in India.

6. Collaboration with Local Authorities:
   o **Collaborate with Local Authorities:** Engage with local regulatory bodies and authorities to stay updated on regional cybersecurity and healthcare regulations.

7. Data Encryption Standards:
   o **AES Encryption:** Implement Advanced Encryption Standard (AES) encryption for protecting sensitive patient data during transmission and storage. AES is recognized as a secure encryption standard.

8. Healthcare Data Sharing:
   o **Data Sharing Agreements:** When sharing patient data with other healthcare providers or institutions, establish data sharing agreements that specify the security measures and data protection practices that all parties must adhere to.

9. Regular Security Audits and Penetration Testing:
    o   **Third-Party Audits:** Consider engaging third-party cybersecurity firms to conduct regular security audits and penetration testing to identify vulnerabilities and ensure compliance with Indian regulations.

10. Patient Consent and Access:
    o   **Informed Consent:** Ensure that patients provide informed consent for the collection, storage, and use of their health information. Clearly explain how their data will be used and protected.
    o   **Patient Access:** Allow patients to access their own health records as per legal requirements. Implement secure authentication methods to verify patients' identities.

11. Incident Reporting:
    o   **Data Breach Reporting:** Familiarize healthcare professionals and staff with the process of reporting data breaches to the Indian Computer Emergency Response Team (CERT-In) and affected patients, as required by Indian law.

12. Secure Healthcare Apps:
    o   **Mobile App Security:** If healthcare apps are used to interact with patients or store health data, ensure that these apps follow secure development practices and encryption standards.

13. Health Insurance Portability and Accountability Act (HIPAA):
    o   **HIPAA Compliance:** While HIPAA is a U.S. regulation, some healthcare professionals and organizations in India may deal with international patients or partners subject to HIPAA. In such cases, consider aligning practices with HIPAA requirements.

It's crucial for healthcare professionals in India to remain compliant with national and state-specific regulations while also adopting international best practices for cybersecurity. Collaboration with legal and cybersecurity experts who specialize in Indian healthcare regulations can be invaluable in navigating the complex landscape of healthcare data protection in the country.

Nonprofit Organizations

Data Protection:

1. **Donor and Beneficiary Data:** Nonprofits often collect and store sensitive donor and beneficiary information, including names, addresses, financial data, and personal stories. Safeguard this data as it's a prime target for cybercriminals.
2. **Encryption:** Use encryption for data both at rest and in transit. This ensures that even if someone gains unauthorized access, they won't be able to decipher the information.
3. **Access Control:** Limit access to sensitive data to authorized personnel only. Implement role-based access controls to ensure that employees or volunteers only have access to the data required for their specific tasks.
4. **Data Backups:** Regularly back up your data and store backups offline. This way, even if your systems are compromised, you can recover your data without paying a ransom or suffering significant losses.

Employee Training:

1. **Cybersecurity Awareness:** Train employees and volunteers about cybersecurity best practices. Make them aware of common threats like phishing, social engineering, and malware.
2. **Incident Response:** Develop and communicate an incident response plan. Ensure that your team knows what to do in case of a data breach or cyberattack to minimize potential damage.

Third-Party Vendors:

- **Vendor Assessment:** If you work with third-party vendors for services like payment processing or donor management, ensure they have robust cybersecurity practices. Conduct regular security assessments and audits of these vendors.

Secure Communication:

1. **Email Security:** Use email encryption and authentication methods like DMARC, SPF, and DKIM to protect against email spoofing and phishing attempts. Train your staff to recognize phishing emails.

2. **Secure Collaboration Tools:** If your team uses collaboration tools, make sure they are secure and use end-to-end encryption for sensitive communications.

Regular Updates:

1. **Software and Systems:** Keep your software, operating systems, and security tools up to date with the latest patches and updates. Cybercriminals often target vulnerabilities in outdated software.
Strong Password Policies:

2. **Password Management:** Enforce strong password policies for all accounts. Encourage the use of complex passwords and the frequent changing of passwords.

Cyber Insurance:

- **Consider Cyber Insurance:** Depending on your organization's size and budget, consider investing in cyber insurance. It can provide financial protection in case of a data breach or cyber incident.

Legal Compliance:

- **Data Protection Laws:** Be aware of and compliant with data protection laws in your region, such as the General Data Protection Regulation (GDPR) in Europe or data protection regulations in India.

Regular Security Audits:

- **Periodic Assessments:** Conduct regular security audits and vulnerability assessments to identify and mitigate potential weaknesses in your cybersecurity posture.

Remember, cybersecurity is an ongoing effort. Even with limited resources, nonprofits can significantly enhance their cybersecurity by following these practices, which will help protect valuable data and maintain the trust of donors and beneficiaries.

Teenagers and Students

Online Privacy and Social Media:

1. **Guard Your Digital Diary:** Your online presence is like a diary. Make sure only trusted friends have access to your personal information. Use privacy settings to control who can see your posts and details.
2. **Public vs. Private:** Think of social media as a big gathering. You chat openly with friends but wouldn't share personal secrets with everyone. Be mindful of what you share publicly and what you keep among close friends.
3. **Digital Footprints:** Imagine your online actions as footprints in the sand; they can last a long time. Before you post something, ask yourself if you'd be comfortable with teachers, parents, or future employers seeing it someday.
4. **Location Sharing:** Consider turning off location sharing when you post updates or pictures. You don't want the whole world to know where you are all the time, right?
5. **Be Cautious with Selfies:** While selfies are fun, be careful about sharing too many. Some bad actors might misuse them.

Safe Online Interactions:

1. **No Room for Cyberbullying:** Just like you wouldn't tolerate bullying in the real world, don't engage with online bullies. Block them, report their behavior, and let a trusted adult know what's happening.
2. **Stranger Danger:** Online, just like in real life, don't chat with strangers. Be cautious about who you interact with, and never give out personal information to people you haven't met in person.
3. **Spot Phishing Attempts:** Be aware of phishing attempts. If someone you don't know asks for personal information, like your password or home address, it's a red flag.

Passwords:

1. **Forge Strong Shields:** Think of your passwords as superhero shields. They need to be strong and unique. Use a mix of letters, numbers, and symbols to create them. Don't use easily guessable information like your birthday or "password123."
2. **Password Manager Magic:** Managing multiple passwords can be tough. Consider using a password manager app to securely store and organize them for you.
3. **Change Passwords Regularly:** Don't use the same password for everything, and change them periodically. This way, if one account is compromised, the rest stay safe.

Downloads and Sharing:

1. **Avoid Shady Links:** Just as you'd think twice about taking candy from a stranger, be cautious about clicking on strange links or downloading files from unfamiliar sources. They could harm your devices or swipe your info.
2. **Keep Things Updated:** Regularly update your devices and apps. These updates often include security improvements that keep you safe from online threats.
3. **Your Online Rep:** Remember, your online actions can stick with you. Be responsible and kind online, as your digital reputation can follow you for a long time.

4. **Speak Up:** If something online makes you uneasy or worried, don't hesitate to talk to a trusted adult about it. They can help you navigate any online issues.

5. **Learn to Identify Fake News:** In the era of information overload, it's important to learn how to spot fake news and verify information before accepting it as fact.

Being tech-savvy is excellent, but it's also vital to be cyber-smart. Protect your privacy, your digital reputation, and your future by following these guidelines. Safely explore the digital world, make the most of the opportunities it offers, and have a great time while you're at it.

Each persona faces unique cybersecurity challenges, and addressing these challenges requires tailored approaches and continuous education. By promoting cyber awareness and implementing best practices, individuals and groups can navigate the digital world securely and protect their online assets and privacy. Additionally, various cybersecurity companies, such as Panoplia.io, offer solutions and services tailored to the needs of different personas, helping them stay safe in the digital realm. Collaborative efforts among individuals, organizations, and cybersecurity providers are crucial in creating a safer digital environment for everyone.

Chapter 7

EMERGING THREATS AND FUTURE TRENDS

Artificial Intelligence and Its Dual Role

Expanding further on the dual role of artificial intelligence (AI), its benefits, and emerging threats:

Positive Implications of AI:

1. **Efficient Resource Management:** AI can optimize resource allocation in sectors like energy and agriculture, leading to reduced waste and enhanced sustainability.
2. **Financial Services:** AI-driven algorithms can improve fraud detection, risk assessment, and investment strategies in the financial industry.
3. **Education Enhancement:** AI-powered educational tools offer personalized learning experiences, helping students of varying abilities excel.
4. **Scientific Discovery:** AI accelerates scientific research by analyzing vast datasets, assisting in drug discovery, and predicting environmental changes.

Emerging Threats and Risks:

1. **AI-Powered Cyberattacks:** Cybercriminals employ AI to automate tasks like scanning for vulnerabilities, crafting convincing phishing emails, and evading traditional security measures. AI-driven attacks are more adaptable and difficult to detect.
2. **Deepfake Technology:** AI-generated deepfakes have the potential to deceive individuals by creating highly convincing fake videos and audio recordings. These can be exploited for various malicious purposes, including spreading false information, blackmail, and impersonation.

3. **Automated Phishing Attacks:** AI-enhanced phishing campaigns can analyze vast amounts of data to craft highly targeted messages. These messages appear more legitimate, increasing the chances of recipients falling victim to scams.

3. **Biased Algorithms:** AI systems learn from historical data, which may contain biases. These biases can be perpetuated by AI algorithms, leading to discriminatory outcomes in areas like hiring, lending, and criminal justice. Addressing algorithmic bias is crucial for fairness and equity.

4. **Privacy Concerns:** AI can process vast amounts of personal data for various purposes, including surveillance, recommendation systems, and user profiling. This raises significant privacy concerns, necessitating robust data protection regulations and practices.

5. **Job Displacement:** The automation of tasks by AI and robotics may lead to job displacement in certain industries, requiring reskilling and workforce adaptation.

6. **Ethical Dilemmas:** The use of AI in autonomous weapons and decision-making raises ethical questions about responsibility and accountability in cases of unintended harm.

Strategies to Address AI-Related Threats:

1. **Advanced Cybersecurity:** Enhance cybersecurity measures by integrating AI-powered tools for threat detection, intrusion prevention, and anomaly detection. Cybersecurity teams must stay updated with evolving AI-driven attack techniques.

2. **Deepfake Detection:** Develop and deploy deepfake detection technologies to identify manipulated content. Combining AI and blockchain can create tamper-proof records of media authenticity.

3. **AI for Good:** Promote the ethical use of AI for societal benefits, such as healthcare, education, and environmental sustainability, while ensuring responsible AI practices.

4. **Algorithmic Fairness:** Implement fairness-aware AI algorithms and conduct regular audits to identify and mitigate biases in AI systems.

5. **Privacy Protection:** Strengthen data protection regulations and promote transparency in AI systems, including clear user consent, data anonymization, and secure data storage.
6. **Education and Awareness:** Raise awareness about AI-related threats among the general public, policymakers, and organizations. Offer training programs to build a workforce capable of addressing AI challenges.
7. **Ethical Guidelines:** Develop and adhere to ethical guidelines for AI development, deployment, and decision-making to ensure responsible AI governance.
8. **Collaboration:** Foster international collaboration to address global AI challenges, including cybersecurity threats, ethical dilemmas, and policy frameworks.
9. **Regulation:** Implement regulatory frameworks that strike a balance between innovation and safeguarding against AI-related risks. These regulations should cover areas like data privacy, autonomous systems, and algorithmic transparency.
10. **Research and Innovation:** Encourage ongoing research and innovation in AI ethics, security, and risk mitigation to stay ahead of emerging threats.

Addressing the dual role of AI requires a multidimensional approach that harnesses its potential for positive transformation while proactively mitigating emerging threats and ethical concerns. Collaboration between governments, businesses, academia, and civil society is essential to ensure responsible and secure AI development and deployment.

Defending Against AI-Driven Threats

1. **AI-Powered Cybersecurity:** Just as AI can be used for malicious purposes, it can also be harnessed to enhance cybersecurity measures. AI-driven tools can quickly identify anomalies, detect threats, and respond in real-time.
2. **Advanced Authentication:** AI can improve authentication processes through biometric recognition, reducing the risk of unauthorized access.
3. **Algorithm Transparency:** Ensuring transparency in AI algorithms can help identify and correct biases, reducing discriminatory outcomes.

4. **Regulation and Governance:** Governments and organizations need to establish regulations and guidelines for the ethical and responsible use of AI.

The Future of AI in Cybersecurity:

The relationship between AI and cybersecurity is dynamic and ever-evolving. As AI technology advances, it will play a pivotal role in shaping the future of cybersecurity:

1. **Predictive Threat Detection:** AI can anticipate potential threats by analyzing vast amounts of data, enabling proactive threat mitigation.
2. **Behavioral Analytics:** AI-driven behavioral analytics can identify unusual patterns of behavior, detecting insider threats and other anomalies.
3. **Automated Responses:** AI-powered systems can autonomously respond to threats, minimizing human intervention and reducing response times.
4. **Adversarial Machine Learning:** Researchers are exploring the use of AI to create defenses against adversarial attacks that attempt to fool AI systems.

Ethical Considerations: Striking a Balance:

While AI brings remarkable advancements, it also raises ethical considerations. Striking a balance between innovation and ethical use is paramount. Transparency, accountability, and collaboration among stakeholders are crucial to harnessing AI's potential for the greater good.

Conclusion: Embracing AI's Potential:

As we navigate the complex landscape of AI, it's essential to recognize its dual role. By embracing AI's potential while remaining vigilant about emerging threats, we can harness its power to drive positive transformations across industries. The future of AI in cybersecurity holds promises of smarter defense mechanisms, enhanced threat detection, and a more resilient digital world. It's our collective responsibility to ensure that AI is wielded ethically and responsibly, paving the way for a secure and prosperous future.

Internet of Things (IoT) Vulnerabilities: Navigating the Connected Landscape

In the era of digital transformation, the concept of the Internet of Things (IoT) has emerged as a transformative force, connecting devices and objects to the internet, enabling them to communicate and share data seamlessly. From smart homes to industrial machinery, IoT has the potential to revolutionize various domains. However, with this connectivity comes a host of vulnerabilities that can compromise security and privacy on an unprecedented scale. In this exploration of IoT vulnerabilities, we delve into the challenges, risks, and potential solutions that arise in the connected landscape.

The Dawn of IoT: A Network of Possibilities

The proliferation of IoT devices has created a network of interconnected entities that can communicate, gather data, and perform actions remotely. From wearable fitness trackers to smart thermostats, these devices enhance convenience and efficiency. However, the very characteristics that make IoT desirable also make it susceptible to vulnerabilities.

Vulnerabilities in IoT: An Array of Challenges:

1. **Weak Authentication:** Many IoT devices lack robust authentication mechanisms, making them vulnerable to unauthorized access.
2. **Lack of Encryption:** Data transmitted between devices is often inadequately encrypted, potentially exposing sensitive information.
3. **Outdated Software:** IoT devices may not receive regular software updates, leaving them vulnerable to known security flaws.
4. **Inadequate Privacy Controls:** Data collected by IoT devices, especially those in homes, may be accessed without the user's consent or knowledge.
5. **Compromised Firmware:** Attackers can manipulate IoT device firmware to gain control or access sensitive information.

Real-World Examples:

1. **Mirai Botnet:** In 2016, the Mirai botnet exploited default usernames and passwords on IoT devices, launching large-scale distributed denial-of-service (DDoS) attacks that disrupted major websites.
2. **Baby Monitor Vulnerabilities:** Security researchers discovered that certain baby monitors lacked encryption, allowing unauthorized individuals to access live feeds of nurseries.
3. **Connected Cars:** Vulnerabilities in IoT-enabled vehicles can potentially allow hackers to remotely control critical functions, compromising driver safety.

Mitigating IoT Vulnerabilities:

1. **Authentication and Authorization:** Implementing strong authentication and authorization mechanisms can prevent unauthorized access to IoT devices.
2. **Encryption:** Ensuring end-to-end encryption for data transmitted between devices can protect against eavesdropping.
3. **Regular Updates:** Manufacturers should provide regular software updates to patch security vulnerabilities and enhance device resilience.
4. **Privacy by Design:** IoT devices should prioritize user privacy by incorporating data protection and user consent features.
5. **Network Segmentation:** Isolating IoT devices from critical networks can limit the potential impact of a breach.

The Role of AI and Machine Learning

Artificial intelligence (AI) and machine learning (ML) are emerging as valuable tools in detecting and mitigating IoT vulnerabilities. These technologies can analyze patterns, detect anomalies, and predict potential threats, enhancing cybersecurity measures.

Looking Ahead: Challenges and Solutions:

As IoT continues to expand its footprint, stakeholders must collaboratively address its vulnerabilities:

1. **Regulation and Standards:** Governments and industry bodies must establish regulations and standards that promote security by design in IoT devices.

2. **Consumer Education:** Educating users about the risks and best practices of IoT usage can empower them to make informed decisions.
3. **Collaboration:** IoT manufacturers, cybersecurity experts, and policymakers must collaborate to develop comprehensive security solutions.

Conclusion: Navigating the IoT Landscape Securely

The allure of IoT lies in its potential to reshape industries, enhance convenience, and improve efficiency. However, the proliferation of connected devices introduces a new realm of vulnerabilities that demand careful consideration. By adopting robust security practices, embracing technological innovations, and promoting awareness, we can harness the power of IoT while mitigating its inherent risks. As IoT continues to evolve, the quest for secure and connected experiences will shape the future of technology and our digital interactions.

Deepfake Technology and Its Implications: Navigating the Age of Synthetic Realities

In an era characterized by rapid technological advancements, deepfake technology has emerged as a powerful and controversial tool that blurs the lines between reality and fabrication. Deepfakes are highly convincing and often indistinguishable videos or audio recordings that use artificial intelligence (AI) to manipulate or replace existing content with fabricated elements. While the technology showcases the potential of AI, it also raises profound ethical, societal, and security concerns. In this exploration of deepfake technology, we delve into its mechanisms, implications, and the challenges it poses to truth and trust.

Unveiling the Mechanics of Deepfakes

Deepfakes are created using complex AI algorithms known as Generative Adversarial Networks (GANs). GANs consist of two neural networks - a generator and a discriminator - that work in tandem to produce increasingly realistic content. The generator creates fake content, while the discriminator attempts to distinguish between real and fake material. As this cycle continues, the generated content becomes progressively more convincing.

Implications for Disinformation and Fake News:

Deepfakes have the potential to upend the way we perceive information and reality:

1. **Political Manipulation:** Deepfakes can be used to manipulate political narratives by altering speeches or videos of public figures, potentially impacting elections and public opinion.
2. **Discrediting Individuals:** False videos can tarnish reputations or spread false information about individuals, leading to personal and professional harm.
3. **Fake Evidence:** Deepfakes can be presented as evidence in legal proceedings, creating new challenges for the justice system.

Ethical and Societal Concerns:

The proliferation of deepfake technology brings forth a range of ethical dilemmas:

1. **Consent and Privacy:** Using someone's likeness without consent raises concerns about privacy and the right to control one's image.
2. **Credibility and Trust:** The erosion of trust in visual and audio content challenges our ability to discern real from fabricated.
3. **Manipulation of Truth:** Deepfakes can be used to create false historical events, eroding the very foundation of truth.

Security Implications:

Deepfakes also pose security risks:

1. **Corporate Sabotage:** Companies could fall victim to deepfake attacks targeting their executives, causing financial damage or data breaches.
2. **Impersonation:** Fraudulent impersonation through deepfakes could lead to unauthorized access to secure systems.

Countering Deepfake Threats:

Several strategies are being developed to mitigate the impact of deepfakes:

1. **Authentication Technology:** Developing tools that can verify the authenticity of media content.

2. **Media Literacy:** Educating the public to critically assess media content and recognize potential manipulations.

3. **Forensic Tools:** Creating AI-powered forensic tools that can detect signs of manipulation in media.

Balancing Innovation and Ethics:
The development of deepfake technology underscores the importance of striking a balance between innovation and ethical considerations. As AI continues to evolve, so do the challenges associated with its use. The responsibility lies not just with developers, but with society as a whole to collectively address the ethical and societal implications of these advancements.

Conclusion: Navigating the Synthetic Reality Landscape
The emergence of deepfake technology heralds a new era in our relationship with reality, posing complex challenges that extend beyond technology itself. As we grapple with the implications of synthetic realities, it becomes essential to foster a global conversation that brings together technologists, policymakers, ethicists, and the public. By addressing the potential harms and exploring ways to harness the power of AI responsibly, we can navigate the evolving landscape of deepfakes while safeguarding the core tenets of truth, trust, and authenticity.

Quantum Computing and Its Effect on Cybersecurity: Shaping the Future of Digital Defense
In the realm of technological innovation, few breakthroughs have captured the imagination quite like quantum computing. Promising to revolutionize the very foundation of computing, quantum computers leverage the principles of quantum mechanics to perform calculations at speeds that defy the capabilities of classical computers. However, with great power comes great responsibility, and the advent of quantum computing also ushers in a new era of cybersecurity challenges. In this exploration, we delve into the intricacies of quantum computing, its potential implications for cybersecurity, and the strategies being devised to secure the digital landscape in the quantum age.

Unveiling the Quantum World

Unlike classical computers that use bits to represent information as either 0 or 1, quantum computers harness quantum bits or qubits. Qubits exist in a superposition, meaning they can represent both 0 and 1 simultaneously. This property enables quantum computers to perform complex calculations with extraordinary speed and efficiency, promising breakthroughs in fields from cryptography to pharmaceuticals.

Shattering Cryptographic Foundations:

Quantum computing has the potential to disrupt traditional cryptographic methods:

1. **Public Key Cryptography:** Quantum computers could swiftly factor large numbers, breaking encryption algorithms like RSA and disrupting secure communication.
2. **Digital Signatures:** Quantum computers could forge digital signatures, jeopardizing the authenticity of digital transactions.

Post-Quantum Cryptography:

In response to the quantum threat, the field of post-quantum cryptography is emerging. This involves developing encryption methods that are resistant to quantum attacks:

1. **Lattice-Based Cryptography:** Encryption methods based on mathematical lattices offer resilience against quantum attacks.
2. **Code-Based Cryptography:** Using error-correcting codes to encrypt messages, which quantum computers struggle to decipher.

Quantum Key Distribution:

Quantum cryptography exploits the properties of quantum mechanics to secure communication:

1. **Quantum Key Distribution (QKD):** QKD leverages the principles of quantum entanglement to create unbreakable cryptographic keys.
2. **Quantum-Safe VPNs:** QKD can be used to secure virtual private networks, ensuring data confidentiality in the quantum era.

Cryptanalysis and Quantum Attacks:

Quantum computers can solve certain problems exponentially faster than classical computers, enabling them to break cryptographic protocols:

1. **Shor's Algorithm:** Quantum computers could factor large numbers, breaking RSA encryption.
2. **Grover's Algorithm:** Quantum computers could search unsorted databases at an exponential speed, impacting symmetric encryption.

Preparing for the Quantum Future:

To secure the digital landscape in the quantum age, organizations and governments are taking proactive measures:

1. **Research and Development:** Investing in quantum-safe cryptographic methods to prepare for the impending quantum threat.
2. **Quantum-Safe Protocols:** Implementing quantum-safe encryption methods to ensure data security.
3. **Quantum Key Distribution:** Deploying QKD technologies to establish secure communication channels.

The Quantum Cybersecurity Landscape:

As quantum computing advances, it promises to unlock unprecedented computational capabilities while simultaneously challenging the foundations of cybersecurity. The transition to quantum-safe cryptography will require collaboration between researchers, businesses, and governments to ensure a secure digital future. By embracing innovation, developing resilient cryptographic methods, and staying ahead of emerging threats, we can navigate the quantum age while preserving the integrity and confidentiality of our digital world.

Chapter 8

CASE STUDIES AND REAL-LIFE STORIES

High-Profile Cyber Frauds and Their Impact

The digital age has brought unparalleled convenience and connectivity, but it has also given rise to a new breed of criminals - cybercriminals. With their sophisticated tactics and insidious schemes, these individuals have managed to breach the digital fortresses of even the most secure organizations and individuals. In this chapter, we delve into a series of high-profile cyber frauds, dissecting their strategies, unraveling their impact, and drawing important lessons for individuals and businesses alike.

1. **The Equifax Breach:** Unmasking Vulnerabilities
   In 2017, one of the largest credit reporting agencies, Equifax, fell victim to a colossal data breach that exposed the personal information of nearly 147 million people. The attackers exploited a vulnerability in Equifax's web application software, gaining unauthorized access to a treasure trove of sensitive data. This breach underscored the pressing need for robust cybersecurity measures and the dire consequences of underestimating cyber threats.

2. **The Bangladesh Bank Heist:** Hacking the Banking System
   In 2016, cybercriminals executed a daring heist against the Bangladesh Bank, attempting to steal a staggering $1 billion. Using fraudulent SWIFT messages, the attackers gained access to the bank's network and attempted to transfer funds to accounts in the Philippines. The incident revealed the vulnerabilities in the global banking system and the critical importance of safeguarding financial institutions against cyber threats.

3. **The WannaCry Ransomware Attack:** Digital Extortion
The WannaCry ransomware attack of 2017 targeted over 300,000 computers across 150 countries, encrypting users' files and demanding a ransom in Bitcoin for their release. This attack exploited a vulnerability in Microsoft Windows, spreading rapidly and paralyzing critical systems in healthcare, transportation, and more. The incident highlighted the potential societal disruptions that cyber threats can pose and the importance of keeping software updated.

4. **The Target Breach:** Hitting Close to Home
In 2013, retail giant Target fell victim to a cyber attack that exposed the credit card information of over 40 million customers. The attackers infiltrated Target's point-of-sale systems using malware introduced through a third-party vendor. The breach highlighted the interconnectedness of modern supply chains and the need for comprehensive cybersecurity measures that extend beyond an organization's immediate boundaries.

5. **The SolarWinds Attack:** A Supply Chain Nightmare
The SolarWinds attack of 2020 revealed the vulnerability of software supply chains to cyberattacks. Hackers compromised software updates for SolarWinds' Orion platform, which was used by numerous organizations, including government agencies and Fortune 500 companies. This sophisticated attack highlighted the challenges of identifying and mitigating threats that infiltrate trusted software sources.

6. **The Twitter Bitcoin Scam:** Hijacking High-Profile Accounts
In 2020, cybercriminals targeted high-profile Twitter accounts, including those of Elon Musk, Barack Obama, and Bill Gates, in a Bitcoin scam. The attackers gained control of the accounts and posted messages urging users to send Bitcoin, promising to double their investments. The incident illustrated how social engineering and impersonation can exploit trust to facilitate financial fraud.

7. **Paytm Phishing Scam:** A Digital Heist
One of the most infamous cyber frauds in India involved the Paytm phishing scam. Cybercriminals impersonated Paytm customer service representatives and tricked users into revealing their account credentials

and OTPs (One-Time Passwords). The stolen information was used to drain victims' wallets. This incident underscored the importance of user education and the need for vigilant verification of service providers.

8. **MobiKwik Data Breach:** A Privacy Breach
   The MobiKwik data breach compromised the personal data of millions of users, including phone numbers, email addresses, and transaction histories. The breach not only exposed user privacy but also raised concerns about the security practices of digital payment platforms. It prompted a broader conversation about data protection laws and the responsibility of companies to safeguard user information.

9. **Facebook Data Scandal:** The Cambridge Analytica Fallout
   The global Facebook data scandal had far-reaching implications in India as well. The scandal involved the unauthorized harvesting of user data by Cambridge Analytica for political profiling purposes. While Indian users were among the affected, the incident highlighted the intricate relationship between social media, personal data, and privacy rights. It led to increased scrutiny of data-sharing practices and calls for stronger data protection regulations.

10. **IRCTC Tatkal Booking Scam:** Exploiting E-commerce
    The IRCTC Tatkal booking scam exposed vulnerabilities in the Indian Railways' online ticketing system. Fraudsters used automated software to book Tatkal tickets in bulk, creating artificial demand and leaving genuine users stranded. The incident highlighted the need for robust anti-bot measures and underscored the challenges of securing e-commerce platforms against technological manipulations.

11. **Amazon Gift Card Fraud:** Leveraging Trust
    Cybercriminals exploited the trust associated with Amazon gift cards to defraud users. Victims received calls from impostors posing as Amazon representatives, claiming that their accounts had been compromised. The victims were then manipulated into purchasing Amazon gift cards and revealing the card details to the fraudsters. This case emphasized the importance of verifying the authenticity of communication and the dangers of blindly trusting caller information.

12. **Olx Fraud:** Manipulating Online Marketplaces

    The Olx fraud case shed light on the dangers of online marketplaces. Criminals posed as sellers on Olx, advertising products at attractive prices. Once victims expressed interest, they were directed to fake payment portals and duped into transferring money without receiving the promised products. This incident highlighted the need for caution when dealing with online transactions and the significance of verifying the credibility of sellers.

Impact and Lessons Learned:

These high-profile cyber fraud cases have profound implications for both consumers and the broader cybersecurity landscape in India:

- **User Vigilance:** The cases underscore the need for users to remain vigilant, verify the authenticity of communication, and never share sensitive information without confirmation.
- **Regulatory Imperatives:** The incidents have driven conversations about the necessity of robust data protection laws and regulations, urging lawmakers to strengthen safeguards for user data.
- **Corporate Responsibility:** Companies providing digital services need to prioritize data security, adopt stringent authentication measures, and invest in cybersecurity infrastructure to prevent breaches.
- **Education and Awareness:** The cases highlight the importance of cyber literacy and the need to educate users about common scams and fraud tactics.
- **Public-Private Collaboration:** The cases call for collaborative efforts between government agencies, law enforcement, and private companies to combat cybercrime effectively.

While these high-profile cases serve as cautionary tales, they also present opportunities for India to fortify its cybersecurity ecosystem, protect its citizens, and foster a digital landscape characterized by trust and resilience.

Drawing Lessons and Forging Ahead:

These high-profile case studies offer a sobering reminder of the potential consequences of cyber frauds. They underscore the importance of:

- **Robust Cybersecurity Measures:** Organizations and individuals must prioritize cybersecurity, investing in firewalls, encryption, and regular security audits.
- **Vigilance and Awareness:** Recognizing the tactics employed by cybercriminals is crucial to avoiding their traps. Regular training and awareness programs are essential.
- **Collaboration:** Cyber threats are borderless. Cooperation between organizations, industries, and governments is essential to mitigating risks effectively.
- **Regulation and Compliance:** The digital landscape requires updated regulations that hold organizations accountable for safeguarding customer data.

In the ever-evolving realm of cyber threats, these case studies remind us that no entity is immune to cyber attacks. By learning from past mistakes and embracing a proactive approach to cybersecurity, we can collectively forge a safer digital future.

Personal Accounts of Cybercrime Victims: Unveiling the Human Impact

Behind every cybercrime statistic lies a real person, a victim who has experienced the devastating effects of digital deception. The world of cybercrime is not just a faceless realm of codes and algorithms; it's a realm that leaves a lasting impact on individuals, families, and businesses. In this chapter, we delve into personal accounts of cybercrime victims, shedding light on the emotional, financial, and psychological toll that these incidents can take.

1. **Jane's Nightmare:** The Aftermath of Identity Theft
   Jane, a middle-aged professional, woke up one morning to discover that her bank accounts were drained and her credit cards maxed out. She

had fallen prey to identity theft. The criminals had obtained her personal information through a phishing email and had used it to wreak havoc on her financial life. Jane spent months trying to restore her credit, proving her innocence to creditors, and securing her compromised accounts. The experience left her not only financially drained but emotionally scarred, eroding her trust in online transactions.

2. **Mark's Digital Double:** Social Media Impersonation
   Mark, a university student, found his life turned upside down when a fake social media profile bearing his name and photos emerged. The imposter used the fake profile to send inappropriate messages to Mark's friends and family, tarnishing his reputation. Mark's real accounts were compromised, and he struggled to regain control over his digital identity. The incident not only damaged his personal relationships but also highlighted the ease with which cybercriminals can manipulate social media to cause harm.

3. **Sarah's E-Commerce Disaster:** Falling for Online Shopping Fraud
   Sarah, an avid online shopper, came across an irresistible deal on a popular e-commerce website. She ordered a high-end gadget, paid in advance, and eagerly awaited its arrival. However, the package that arrived contained a cheap imitation. Sarah had fallen victim to an online shopping scam. Her attempts to contact the seller went unanswered, and she realized she had lost both her money and her trust in online shopping platforms. The incident served as a stark reminder that even reputable platforms can host fraudulent listings.

4. **A Small Business's Struggle:** Ransomware Attack
   A small accounting firm became the target of a ransomware attack that encrypted their critical client data. The attackers demanded a hefty ransom in exchange for the decryption key. The business owner, faced with the dilemma of losing essential data or paying the ransom, chose the latter. While the decryption key worked, the incident not only cost the business financially but also eroded client trust and tarnished the firm's reputation. The attack underscored the vulnerabilities small businesses face in the digital landscape.

Lessons from Victims:

These personal accounts underscore the far-reaching consequences of cybercrime beyond the confines of digital realms. They highlight the importance of:

- **Vigilance and Education:** Equipping individuals with the knowledge to recognize and respond to cyber threats is paramount. Cyber literacy can empower users to make informed decisions and avoid falling into traps.
- **Preventive Measures:** Regularly updating passwords, enabling two-factor authentication, and verifying sources before sharing personal information can prevent many cybercrimes.
- **Emotional Support:** Victims often experience feelings of violation, anxiety, and helplessness. Providing emotional support and resources to navigate the aftermath is crucial.
- **Public Awareness:** Sharing personal accounts can drive home the reality of cyber threats, encouraging others to take cybersecurity seriously.

While the personal stories of victims reveal the darker side of the digital world, they also serve as a rallying cry for collective action against cybercrime. Through education, prevention, and support, individuals can reclaim control over their digital lives and contribute to a safer online environment.

Successful Cybercrime Investigations in India

In the realm of cyberspace, where anonymity often prevails and virtual trails can vanish in an instant, successful cybercrime investigations are no small feat. India, a country with a rapidly growing digital footprint, has been witnessing a surge in cybercrimes. From financial frauds to data breaches, cybercriminals have been capitalizing on vulnerabilities in the digital infrastructure. In response, law enforcement agencies, cybersecurity experts, and legal authorities have been working tirelessly to unravel the intricacies of cybercrimes and bring the perpetrators to justice.

Challenges in Cybercrime Investigations

Investigating cybercrimes presents unique challenges that set them apart from traditional crimes. Digital evidence can be easily manipulated or erased, the physical location of perpetrators might be obscured, and the global nature of the internet complicates jurisdictional matters. In India, cybercrime investigations encounter additional hurdles, including the lack of comprehensive legislation, a shortage of cybercrime experts, and the constantly evolving tactics of cybercriminals.

Chapter 9

BUILDING A SECURE DIGITAL FUTURE

In an era defined by rapid technological advancement, building a secure digital future has become paramount. The current generation, and those to come, are growing up in an interconnected world where digital technology is woven into the fabric of everyday life. Ensuring a secure digital future involves not only safeguarding against cyber threats but also fostering responsible digital citizenship and ethical behavior. This chapter explores the key principles and strategies for building a secure digital future for the current generation and generations to come.

1. **Digital Literacy:** Nurturing Informed Users

   Building a secure digital future begins with digital literacy. It's essential to educate individuals from an early age about the digital landscape, online risks, and safe practices. Digital literacy empowers individuals to make informed decisions, recognize potential threats, and protect themselves online. Educational institutions, parents, and guardians play a pivotal role in imparting these skills. Topics covered should include:

   o **Cybersecurity Awareness:** Teaching individuals to identify common threats like phishing, malware, and scams.

   o **Privacy Protection:** Educating about online privacy, data protection, and the responsible use of personal information.

   o **Critical Thinking:** Encouraging critical evaluation of online content and promoting media literacy to combat misinformation.

   o **Ethical Behavior:** Fostering an understanding of digital ethics, including responsible social media use and online conduct.

2. **Cybersecurity Hygiene:** Practicing Safe Habits

   Promoting cybersecurity hygiene is fundamental to building a secure digital future. Individuals should adopt and maintain good digital habits to reduce vulnerabilities. Emphasize the following practices:

   o **Strong Passwords:** Encourage the use of complex, unique passwords for online accounts and the regular updating of passwords.

   o **Multi-Factor Authentication (MFA):** Stress the importance of enabling MFA wherever possible to enhance account security.

   o **Software Updates:** Emphasize the significance of keeping operating systems, applications, and security software up to date to patch vulnerabilities.

   o **Safe Browsing:** Teach safe browsing habits, including avoiding suspicious websites and downloads.

   o **Secure Communication:** Promote the use of encrypted messaging and email services to protect sensitive communications.

3. **Ethical Digital Citizenship:** Nurturing Responsibility

   A secure digital future is not solely about technical measures; it's also about fostering ethical digital citizenship. Encourage responsible online behavior and interactions:

   o **Respect for Others:** Promote respectful and empathetic communication online, addressing cyberbullying and harassment.

   o **Intellectual Property:** Teach respect for intellectual property rights, including copyrights and plagiarism avoidance.

   o **Digital Footprint:** Educate individuals about the concept of a digital footprint, highlighting the importance of a positive online presence.

   o **Online Accountability:** Stress the consequences of online actions and the accountability that comes with them.

4. **Secure Technologies:** Advancing Innovation with Safety

   To build a secure digital future, technology developers and innovators must prioritize security from the outset. This involves:

   o **Security by Design:** Embedding security features into digital products and services during their development.

   o **Data Protection:** Implementing robust data protection measures, including encryption and privacy-by-design principles.

- o **Regular Auditing:** Conducting security audits and assessments to identify and address vulnerabilities proactively.
- o **Regulatory Compliance:** Adhering to data protection and cybersecurity regulations to ensure user privacy and security.

5. **Collaborative Efforts:** Partnerships for a Secure Future

A secure digital future is a collective effort that involves collaboration among individuals, organizations, and governments:

- o **Public-Private Partnerships:** Encouraging cooperation between governments, businesses, and civil society to combat cyber threats and share threat intelligence.
- o **Information Sharing:** Promoting the sharing of cybersecurity information and best practices within communities and across industries.
- o **Government Initiatives:** Supporting government initiatives aimed at enhancing national cybersecurity and protecting critical infrastructure.

6. **Adaptability and Continual Learning:** Staying Ahead

Cyber threats constantly evolve, making adaptability and continuous learning critical. Instill the importance of staying informed about emerging threats and adopting new security measures:

- o **Lifelong Learning:** Encourage a mindset of lifelong learning in the digital realm, keeping pace with evolving technologies and threats.
- o **Security Training:** Provide regular cybersecurity training and awareness programs to individuals and organizations.
- o **Incident Response:** Develop incident response plans to effectively address and mitigate cyber incidents when they occur.

7. **Global Cooperation:** A Unified Approach

Building a secure digital future transcends borders. International cooperation is essential to combatting global cyber threats. Nations should work together to:

- o **International Agreements:** Promote and adhere to international agreements and norms related to cyberspace security.
- o **Global Standards:** Establish global cybersecurity standards and best practices for the benefit of all nations.
- o **Cyber Diplomacy:** Engage in diplomatic efforts to address cyber conflicts and promote stability in cyberspace.

By instilling digital literacy, cybersecurity hygiene, ethical digital citizenship, and fostering innovation and collaboration, we can pave the way for a secure digital future that benefits everyone, both today and in the generations to come. Building this future is not only a technical endeavor but also a societal responsibility, requiring the collective efforts of individuals, communities, organizations, and nations.

The Role of Law Enforcement Agencies

Despite these challenges, Indian law enforcement agencies have made significant strides in conducting successful cybercrime investigations. The Cyber Crime Cell (CCC) of the Indian police, along with specialized units like the Cyber Crime Investigation Units (CCIU), has been at the forefront of combating cybercrimes. These units collaborate with other law enforcement agencies, such as the Central Bureau of Investigation (CBI) and the Intelligence Bureau (IB), to create a coordinated response to cyber threats.

Case Studies:

1. The Shifu Trojan Investigation: The investigation into the Shifu Trojan case showcased India's ability to collaborate with international agencies. The Trojan targeted banking institutions and compromised user credentials, resulting in significant financial losses. Law enforcement agencies collaborated with cybersecurity firms to identify the malware's origin and track its operators, leading to multiple arrests.

2. The Unocoin Bitcoin ATM Scam: This investigation highlighted the interconnectedness of digital currency and cybercrime. Fraudsters exploited a cryptocurrency company's branding to set up a fake Bitcoin ATM. Law enforcement authorities, equipped with technological tools and insights from blockchain experts, unraveled the scheme and arrested the culprits.

3. The Matka Gambling Racket: The cyber investigation into the online Matka gambling racket demonstrated how law enforcement agencies can tackle not only high-tech cybercrimes but also traditional illegal activities using digital means. The investigation tracked the flow of money, identified key players, and led to the disruption of the gambling network.

4. The Arrest of 'Dreaded Bunny': The 'Dreaded Bunny' case exemplifies the international dimension of cybercrime investigations. The arrest of a hacker who targeted US organizations involved coordinated efforts between Indian agencies and the Federal Bureau of Investigation (FBI). The collaboration demonstrated the global reach of cybercriminals and the importance of international cooperation.

Key Success Factors:

- **Digital Forensics Expertise:** The advancement of digital forensics tools and techniques has enabled investigators to extract crucial evidence from digital devices and networks, aiding in building strong cases against cybercriminals.
- **Public Awareness Campaigns:** Law enforcement agencies have collaborated with cybersecurity firms and government bodies to raise awareness about cyber threats. These campaigns educate the public about common scams and methods of prevention.
- **International Collaboration:** Cybercrime is borderless, necessitating cooperation between countries. India has participated in international initiatives, such as Interpol's Cyber Fusion Center, to share intelligence and insights on cybercrimes.
- **Legislative Improvements:** India has been working on strengthening its legal framework related to cybercrimes. The Information Technology (Amendment) Act, 2008, introduced provisions related to cybercrimes, but continuous updates are essential to stay ahead of evolving threats.

The Way Forward

Successful cybercrime investigations underscore the importance of continuous adaptation and collaboration. Law enforcement agencies need to continually upgrade their skills, leverage advanced technologies, and strengthen partnerships with cybersecurity experts and international counterparts. Moreover, the development of a robust legal framework that comprehensively addresses cybercrimes and facilitates investigations is imperative.

As the world's digital landscape continues to expand, the battle against cybercrime will remain an ongoing challenge. However, the successes achieved so far are indicative of the nation's determination to safeguard its digital citizens and create a secure online environment.

Corporate Responsibility and Cybersecurity

In an age where digital technology pervades every aspect of business operations, the importance of cybersecurity has risen to unprecedented levels. As organizations increasingly rely on technology to store, process, and transmit sensitive data, the potential risks and repercussions of cyber threats have grown substantially. In response, the concept of corporate responsibility in the realm of cybersecurity has gained traction, emphasizing the need for proactive education and awareness initiatives.

Understanding Corporate Responsibility in Cybersecurity:
Corporate responsibility in the context of cybersecurity goes beyond mere compliance with regulations. It entails a commitment to safeguarding not only the organization's proprietary information but also the personal and financial data of customers and clients. It involves adopting a proactive stance towards cybersecurity, recognizing that the ramifications of a cyber breach can extend far beyond financial losses to include reputational damage, legal liabilities, and erosion of customer trust.

The Role of Cybersecurity Education and Awareness

Cybersecurity education and awareness form the foundation of any effective corporate responsibility strategy. These initiatives empower employees, stakeholders, and customers with the knowledge and tools to recognize, prevent, and respond to cyber threats. By fostering a culture of cyber hygiene, organizations can significantly reduce their susceptibility to attacks and mitigate potential damages.

Empowering Employees

1. **Cyber Hygiene Workshops:** Regular workshops on cyber hygiene practices, including password management, phishing detection, and secure data handling, can equip employees with essential skills to protect themselves and the organization.
2. **Incident Response Training:** Educating employees about the steps to take in case of a cyber incident can minimize the impact of breaches and help in swift containment and recovery.

Building Customer Trust

1. **Transparency:** Organizations can demonstrate their commitment to cybersecurity by openly sharing their security practices, policies, and incident response plans with customers. Transparency cultivates trust and reassures customers that their data is in safe hands.
2. **Customer Education:** Regular communication with customers about prevalent cyber threats, such as phishing scams and social engineering, can empower them to stay vigilant and make informed decisions online.

Stakeholder Engagement

1. **Vendor and Supplier Awareness:** Organizations should extend their cybersecurity education efforts to vendors and suppliers. A chain is only as strong as its weakest link, and a breach in a partner's system can have far-reaching consequences.
2. **Board-Level Awareness:** The board of directors should have a comprehensive understanding of the organization's cybersecurity posture and strategy. A cyber-aware board can ensure that cybersecurity is integrated into the company's overall risk management framework.

The Business Case for Cybersecurity Education

Investing in cybersecurity education and awareness is not only a moral imperative but also makes sound business sense. A breach can lead to direct financial losses, legal fees, regulatory fines, and reputational damage. The costs associated with remediating a breach far exceed the investment required for proactive education initiatives.

Fostering a Culture of Cybersecurity:

Corporate responsibility in cybersecurity requires the integration of security practices into the fabric of the organization. It involves leadership commitment, resource allocation, and continuous evaluation of the evolving threat landscape. As technology evolves, cybersecurity education and awareness must keep pace to address new challenges such as remote work vulnerabilities, cloud security, and emerging threats like ransomware.

Future of Corporate Responsibility in Cybersecurity:

The future of corporate responsibility in cybersecurity lies in a holistic approach that extends beyond internal operations. Organizations will increasingly be judged by their cybersecurity practices when forming partnerships, attracting customers, and interacting with stakeholders. Governments, regulatory bodies, and consumers alike are demanding transparency, accountability, and demonstrated commitment to cybersecurity.

Cybersecurity education and awareness are integral components of corporate responsibility in the digital age. Organizations that prioritize these initiatives not only protect their own interests but also contribute to the overall security of the digital ecosystem. By cultivating a culture of cyber awareness, organizations can fortify themselves against cyber threats while building trust and resilience in an increasingly interconnected world.

Chapter 10

ARTIFICIAL INTELLIGENCE AND MACHINE LEARNING IN DETECTING FRAUD

In the ever-evolving landscape of cybersecurity, the battle against fraud has reached new frontiers with the integration of artificial intelligence (AI) and machine learning (ML) technologies. These cutting-edge tools have revolutionized fraud detection and prevention, enabling organizations to stay one step ahead of cybercriminals. In this chapter, we delve into the role of AI and ML in the fight against fraud and explore how these technologies are transforming the cybersecurity landscape.

The Rise of AI and ML in Fraud Detection

Artificial intelligence refers to machines' ability to mimic human intelligence, enabling them to analyze data, make decisions, and learn from experience. Machine learning is a subset of AI that focuses on the development of algorithms allowing computers to learn and make predictions based on data patterns. When applied to fraud detection, AI and ML offer a powerful synergy that enhances the accuracy, efficiency, and speed of identifying fraudulent activities.

Key Applications of AI and ML in Fraud Detection:

1. **Anomaly Detection:** AI and ML algorithms excel at identifying unusual patterns in vast datasets. In fraud detection, this means they can quickly detect deviations from the norm, such as atypical spending behavior, irregular transaction times, or unfamiliar locations. By continually learning from historical data, these algorithms adapt to evolving fraud tactics.

2. **Behavioral Analysis:** AI and ML systems can create profiles of user behavior, recognizing what constitutes "normal" for an individual. Any deviations from these profiles can trigger alerts for further investigation. This is particularly valuable in scenarios like account takeover or identity theft.

3. **Natural Language Processing (NLP):** In addition to analyzing structured data, AI-powered NLP techniques can process unstructured data sources, including text and voice communications. By scanning emails, chat logs, and call transcripts, AI can identify language cues that suggest fraudulent activities, such as phishing attempts or social engineering.

4. **Real-Time Fraud Detection:** AI and ML systems operate in real time, enabling instantaneous fraud detection. When a transaction or interaction occurs, these technologies can assess the risk and decide whether to allow, flag, or deny it, all within milliseconds.

AI and ML in the Fight Against Credit Card and UPI Fraud

In the relentless battle against credit card fraud and UPI (Unified Payments Interface) fraud, artificial intelligence (AI) and machine learning (ML) have emerged as powerful allies. These technologies are transforming the way financial institutions, payment providers, and e-commerce platforms detect and prevent fraudulent transactions. Here's how AI and ML are making a difference in combating these types of fraud:

Transaction Monitoring and Anomaly Detection:

- **Pattern Recognition:** AI and ML systems can analyze vast amounts of transaction data to establish patterns of normal behavior for each account holder. Any deviations from these patterns, such as unusual spending patterns or unfamiliar locations, can raise red flags.

- **Real-Time Analysis:** AI and ML algorithms operate in real time, enabling immediate fraud detection. As soon as a transaction occurs, these systems can assess the risk and decide whether to allow or block it.

Behavioral Biometrics:

- **User Profiling:** These technologies can create detailed profiles of user behavior, identifying what is typical for each individual account holder. Suspicious deviations from these profiles, like changes in the device used for transactions, can trigger alerts.
- **Continuous Learning:** AI and ML models continuously update their understanding of user behavior as they analyze new data, adapting to evolving fraud tactics.

Natural Language Processing (NLP):

- **Text and Speech Analysis:** AI-driven NLP techniques can scrutinize text and voice communications to identify linguistic cues indicative of fraudulent activity. For instance, analyzing chat logs, emails, or call transcripts can help detect phishing attempts and social engineering.

Risk Assessment and Decision Making:

- **Risk Scoring:** AI and ML systems assign risk scores to transactions, which can be used to prioritize alerts for manual review. This ensures that high-risk transactions receive immediate attention while low-risk ones proceed without disruption.
- **Automated Decision Making:** In many cases, these technologies can make automated decisions, such as blocking transactions that exhibit high-risk characteristics. This speed is crucial in preventing fraudulent transactions from going through.

Adaptive Defense:

- **Evolving Fraud Detection:** AI and ML models evolve alongside emerging fraud tactics and trends. They continuously learn from new data, improving their detection capabilities and staying one step ahead of fraudsters.

Challenges and Ethical Considerations

While AI and ML offer tremendous benefits in combatting credit card and UPI fraud, they also present challenges. Ensuring data privacy and security is paramount. Additionally, addressing biases in AI algorithms is essential to prevent discrimination in fraud detection.

The Future of AI and ML in Fraud Detection

AI and ML have already proven their worth in the fight against fraud, and their role will only expand. Organizations will continue to invest in these technologies to stay ahead of evolving threats. Additionally, AI and ML will play a crucial role in the development of proactive and predictive fraud prevention solutions, making it even more challenging for cybercriminals to succeed.

The integration of AI and ML into fraud detection represents a significant leap forward in cybersecurity. By leveraging these advanced technologies, organizations can more effectively protect themselves and their customers from the ever-present threat of fraud. However, this ongoing battle also underscores the need for ethical and privacy considerations as we navigate this rapidly evolving landscape.

Chapter 11

NAVIGATING THE DIGITAL WORLD SAFELY

Recap of Key Takeaways

The journey through the intricate landscape of cyber frauds, threats, and preventive measures has unveiled the complex interplay between human vulnerability and technological manipulation. In a world where our lives are increasingly intertwined with the digital realm, the imperative to safeguard our online identity and assets has never been more crucial. As we conclude this exploration, let's recap the key takeaways that can empower us to navigate the digital world safely.

Knowledge is Power

Understanding the modus operandi of cybercriminals is the first line of defense. Recognizing the tactics they employ – be it phishing, social engineering, or malware attacks – empowers us to detect and thwart their advances. Stay informed about the latest cyber threats and educate yourself about the evolving techniques used by cybercriminals.

Trust But Verify

While technology has brought unprecedented convenience to our lives, blind trust can be perilous. Always verify the authenticity of emails, messages, and websites before divulging sensitive information. Pay attention to URLs, grammar errors, and the context of requests. Remember, genuine entities won't ask for sensitive details over email or chat.

Cyber Hygiene Matters

Adopting good cyber hygiene practices is akin to locking your doors before leaving your home. Use strong, unique passwords for each account, enable two-factor authentication, and keep your software and devices updated. Regularly back up your data to protect against ransomware attacks.

Think Twice, Click Once

When in doubt, pause and think before clicking on a link or downloading an attachment. Cybercriminals often exploit our impulsive actions. A moment of hesitation can save you from falling victim to a phishing attack or malware infection.

Educate Your Loved Ones

The elderly and children are particularly vulnerable to cyber threats. Educate your parents, grandparents, and younger family members about online safety. Share tips, techniques, and resources that can help them make informed decisions in the digital world.

Report Suspicious Activity

If you encounter suspicious emails, messages, or websites, report them to the relevant authorities. Reporting cybercrime not only protects you but also contributes to the larger effort to combat online frauds.

Stay Vigilant & Stay Updated

The world of cyber threats is in a perpetual state of flux. Cybercriminals constantly adapt their tactics to exploit new vulnerabilities. Stay updated about the latest cybersecurity trends, news, and solutions. Engage with reputable cybersecurity sources, attend webinars, and participate in workshops to bolster your knowledge.

Leverage Technology

Fortunately, technology is not just a source of cyber threats; it's also a powerful defense mechanism. Utilize antivirus software, firewalls, and security suites to protect your devices from malware and intrusions. Consider using identity theft protection services that monitor your personal information across the web.

Prioritize Privacy

Respect for your own privacy is paramount. Be cautious about sharing personal information on social media platforms and other online forums. Check privacy settings on your social media accounts and limit the information you share with the public. The less cybercriminals know about you, the harder it is for them to exploit your personal data.

Cultivate Cyber Resilience

Despite your best efforts, there's a possibility of encountering cyber threats. Cultivate cyber resilience by regularly backing up your data. This ensures that even if your device is compromised, your valuable information remains intact.

Be the Beacon of Change

The culture of cyber awareness needs champions. Be that champion in your family, workplace, and community. Advocate for cybersecurity education and best practices. Encourage institutions and organizations to prioritize cybersecurity training for their employees and members.

As we bid adieu to this comprehensive exploration of cyber threats and preventive measures, remember that safety in the digital world is not just an option; it's a necessity. By arming ourselves with knowledge, embracing good cyber practices, and fostering a culture of cyber awareness, and having solutions focused on privacy while protecting us from frauds, we can navigate the digital landscape with confidence and protect what matters most — our digital identities and the trust we place in the virtual realm.

In a world where our lives are increasingly conducted online, cybersecurity is not just a choice; it's a responsibility that we all share. Let us embrace this responsibility and work together to make the digital world a safer place for ourselves and future generations.